CORPORATE COMBAT

CORPORATE COMBAT

William E. Peacock

Facts On File Publications
New York, New York ● Bicester, England

This book is dedicated to three Marine Corps second lieutenants who would have done extremely well in applying the Principles of War to business, but for the fact that the names of Bob Miller, Bexar Matocha and Dale Loudin are engraved on the Vietnam War Memorial in Washington, D.C.

CORPORATE COMBAT

Copyright © 1984 by William E. Peacock

Library of Congress Cataloging in Publication Data
Peacock, William E.
   Corporate combat.

   1. Industrial management. 2. Competition.
3. Strategy 4. Tactics. 5. Battles. I. Title.
HD38.P35   1984   658   84-13614
ISBN 0-87196-222-5

Printed in U.S.A.
10 9 8 7 6 5 4 3 2 1

Composition by Centennial Graphics
Book printed by the Maple-Vail
Manufacturing Group

Acknowledgments

Of the many people who encouraged me to write this book, all of whom I thank, there are several who deserve special mention: Bill Proctor, himself an author of many books and a great Marine Corps officer and Harvard Law buddy, who started the whole operation; Bill Adler, who was most convincing that the concept and plan of attack for the book was solid; Bruce Cassiday, without whose splendid logistical efforts CORPORATE COMBAT would not have reached even the staging area; Kate Kelly, my faithful, patient and supportive editor; Ed Knappman, her boss, who allowed and encouraged her to be all of the above; my fellow Hypertat executives, Ted Bakewell III and Mike Jantzen, who supported this effort and now have adopted a semblance of military language if for no other reason than as protective coloring; Bill Clark of the Pentagon, a West Pointer, who so clearly embodies the successful application of the nine principles in his daily life; most importantly, Polly Peacock, the best wife any executive, entrepreneur or soldier could ask for, and the three super kids who gave up some of their time with Dad so this book could be done, Billy, Janie and Sally; and, finally, the institution and state of mind known as the U.S. Marine Corps, which should need no explanation. May God bless and look over all these people as they march forward through life's valleys to climb its soaring peaks.

CONTENTS

Preface

When someone writes a book, people often ask, "Why did you write it?" The usual answer, "I thought it needed to be written," may seem glib. In this case, my answer is identical, but my reason is not glib.

From my corporate and military experience, one thing stands out clearly—the leaders of industry and the military, despite their vastly different backgrounds and philosophies, have successfully applied the nine Principles of War in their professional lives.

Let's look at a few examples:

Robert H. Waterman, a director of the management consulting firm of McKinsey & Co., Inc., is a master at dealing with his top management clients. By applying the Principles of Mass and Economy of Force, he concentrates his team's efforts on those points of business strategy that will have breakthrough importance and he holds in check those strategies that seem easier to implement but contain fewer seeds of future client success. Bob Waterman's book, IN SEARCH OF EXCELLENCE, is a comprehensive statement of his philosophy.

John R. Beckett, the former chairman of Transamerica Corporation, took over what was basically a workout department for bad loans of a major U.S. bank worth $100 million and turned it into a multi-industry giant worth $4 billion. In order to develop the public's recognition of his company, Jack Beckett had to follow the Principle of Objective; he built one of the most fantastic and controversial skyscrapers in America, the Transamerica Pyramid. Anyone who watched the 1984 Olympics knows which company owns the pyramid, but who could name the owner of the Empire State Building or of the World Trade Center?

When Thomas R. Wilcox took over as CEO of the Crocker National Bank in 1974, the bank had shown only slow, lackluster growth for a decade. Wilcox, a former Navy officer, revitalized the entire operation from top to bottom and followed the Principles of Surprise and Security to turn the complacent, essentially noncompetitive California banking industry on its ear. One of dozens of his surprise maneuvers, which he kept under strict security wraps, was the great "Crocker Bear" coup, in which he simultaneously boosted the rate paid on passbook savings from 4½% to 5% and gave anyone who opened a new account a lovable teddy bear. While the stuffier, more staid bankers around the state sniffed, the little bears received nationwide publicity and Crocker's savings deposits soared at the expense of its competitors.

As the first secretary of energy, James R. Schlesinger demonstrated his superb mastery of the Principles of War as he guided the unpopular but vital National Energy Act through Congress. Known for his no-nonsense brilliance, Jim Schlesinger, a former secretary of defense, applied the Principle of Maneuver (among other tactics) to hammer out a series of congressional victories.

About the same time, the first black service secretary, Clifford L. Alexander, was running the U.S. Army. The all-volunteer force, begun under the Ford Administration, was having difficulties meeting its recruiting goals and was under loud criticism, particularly for recruiting too many blacks. Cliff Alexander focused on the Principle of Offense and met the issues head on. He testified before the House Armed Services Committee, along with his chief of staff, Gen. E.C. Meyer, and demonstrated to all but a few that the status and capability of the U.S. Army under his leadership had improved vastly from its post-Vietnam malaise. Cliff Alexander also targeted recruiting in his offense tactics. He authorized and launched the "Be all that you can be" campaign, perhaps the single most successful institutional advertising campaign in the United States. The army's ad agency, N.W. Ayer, received numerous awards, and the general running the recruiting command eventually earned two more stars. He is now the vice chief of staff.

Charles F. Knight is yet another example of a CEO who successfully applied the Principles of War to running his corporation. A recipient of many management-excellence awards—so many, in fact, that the mahogany walls of his office can't be seen for plaques, citations and trophies—Chuck Knight runs, really runs, by sheer force of will, the $3.5 billion industrial conglomerate known as Emerson Electric Co. While Emerson has about 40 separate subsidiaries, not one of 50,000 employees disputes Knight's adherence to the Principle of Unity of Command. While each division president has authority over his own respective operation, Chuck's persuasive and demanding style makes it clear that authority—but not responsibility—can be delegated, yet he delves into the details of his subordinate units' operations like few other chief executives in America. Like the previous chairman, Buck Persons, Knight has an enviable record. In 10 years, he's virtually doubled the size of Emerson while maintaining over 100 quarters of steadily increasing earnings.

So what if these super leaders happen to follow the Principles of War in their endeavors. Why should anyone read this book and, more to the point, who should read it?

There is no attempt in this book to glorify war—it is a horrible experience. While war itself is an ugly truth, the *art* of war is designed to save lives and other resources by using optimal strategies and tactics. Thus the *art* of war requires efficient leadership and realistic objectives. So does the art of business. The point of this book, then, is to demonstrate how the Principles of War, refined for optimal effect over thousands of years, can be applied to the relatively new art of modern business, which is at most 50 to 60 years old. The result is a field guide of time-tested strategy and tactics for any corporate commander.

With the Vietnam War (in which I proudly fought) now 10 years behind us, a new generation of Americans is entering the ranks of middle management with little or no understanding of things military. Either because of antipathy or lack of exposure, this group of men and women will not understand as well as they should what their bosses and their CEOs mean when they speak about "frontal assaults," "defensive perimeters," "penetration tactics," and the like.

Having seen the Principles of War work well in the corporate world, it seems useful to share these ideas with the men and women entering positions of corporate responsibility so that, as in the zero-sum exercise of war, they will have a better chance of surviving and prospering in the tough economic world in which they work.

St. Louis
1984

one

BASICS

War is much too serious a thing to be left to military men.

TALLEYRAND

It is popular in today's sociological climate to separate essential endeavors of humankind into mutually incompatible categories. Two such essentials are the marketing of goods and the waging of war.

From the beginning of recorded time, however, these two basic aspects of human behavior have been inextricably linked.

Granted, war is hell. Fighting is no way to settle an argument. Shedding blood is awful.

A verse from Isaiah puts it best:

> They shall beat their swords into plowshares, and their spears into pruninghooks: nation shall not lift up sword against nation, neither shall they learn war anymore.

FROM MAKING WAR TO MAKING BREAD

Note the link between war and trade. In his allusion to plowshares and to pruninghooks, the biblical writer was recommending the metamorphosis of industry from a wartime to an agricultural—and thus mercantile—orientation. In other words, he was exhorting the populace to put down their arms and pick up their tools of trade. He was telling them to turn away from war and toward commerce.

War and trade were inexorably linked in ancient myth and legend, as well as in biblical writings. The *Iliad* was the legendary tale of the siege of Troy by the Greeks. The *Odyssey* was the legendary tale of the reshaping of the Greek culture from a wartime basis to a peacetime trade basis.

The wanderings of Ulysses in the *Odyssey* have struck historians as allegorical parallels to the opening of trade routes in the Mediterranean area; in other words, they were a kind of port-to-port recounting of the places to which Greek merchants had sailed for trade purposes, woven into a "tale."

"It is probable that in the generation before the historic siege of Troy the Greeks had tried to force their way through the Hellespont and open the Black Sea to colonization and trade," wrote Will Durant in *The Story of Civilization*. "The story of the Argonauts may be the dramatized memory of that commercial exploration; and the 'golden fleece' may refer to the woolen skins or cloths anciently used in northern Asia Minor to catch particles of gold carried down by the streams."

In recent times, since the end of World War II, much has been written about the capability of our former adversaries, Japan and Germany, to substitute their defeats on the battlefield with victory after victory, in industry after industry, in the economic world. For two societies so heavily militarized, to be able to convert so readily to positions of peacetime economic dominance, albeit with considerable assistance from the United States and under our military umbrella, suggests that there may be a connection between their prior military organizations and orientations and their recent trade successes.

PARALLELS BETWEEN WAR AND TRADE

The human race has always fluctuated between marketing goods and waging war. People have been either making money or making fists.

Naturally, philosophers, historians and politicians have noted similarities between the two endeavors.

Friedrich Engels, one of the fathers of modern communism, once wrote to Karl Marx:

> Among other things I am now reading Clausewitz's *On War*. A strange way of philosophizing but very good on his subject. To the question whether war should be called an art or a science, the answer given is that war is most like trade.

And from that answer he concluded:

> Fighting is to war what cash payment is to trade, for however rarely it may be necessary for it actually to occur, everything is directed through it and eventually it must take place all the same and must be decisive.

And John Dryden, in his introduction to the poem "King Arthur," wrote:

> War is the trade of kings.

In a more contemporary vein, Albert W. Emery has written:

> Marketing is merely a civilized form of warfare in which most battles are won by words, ideas, and disciplined thinking.

Not unexpectedly, therefore, in today's business world we see the almost unconscious use of military words and battle phrases in discussions of business strategies—particularly those dealing with marketing techniques.

- One enterprising marketing executive usually refers to his sales personnel as "shock troops." In fact, the word "troops" is used constantly by business executives on all levels to refer to personnel of any kind.
- Another marketing specialist hints broadly at a "new secret weapon" in a coming marketing "skirmish."
- There are "border clashes" and "encounters" in sales maneuvers.

- One executive even has his office door labeled with the huge symbols "G-2" rather than the more mundane phrase "marketing research."
- We talk in business of market "penetration," "outflanking" our competition and. . . .

MILITARY AND CORPORATE STRUCTURES

Although many individuals who are unfamiliar with military operations and the basics of military staff structure may think that the term "table of organization" is a phrase peculiar to the corporate world, it actually comes out of the military manuals, as does another popular term applied to many corporate heads—"chief executive officer," or "CEO."

Actually, it takes very little to equate the functions of industrial organization with those of a military unit—and, for that matter, vice versa. This fact was not lost on the author of the words from the Song of Solomon.

For the moment, let's look at the typical structure of a wartime organization. Starting from the top, here is a brief summary of the purpose and duties of the staff of the high command, beginning with its broad mission:

- to allocate troop units to an operation
- to provide intelligence on the disposition and capabilities of the enemy forces
- to draw up strategic plans
- to estimate the supplies and transport necessary to achieve victory

And so we have:

- personnel
- intelligence
- planning
- supply and transport

For the sake of simplicity, the military numbers these four functions 1 through 4. And so a general's staff is divided functionally into four separate sections to handle these tasks, with each headed by a senior officer, indicated by the "G." Thus:

G-1:   personnel
G-2:   intelligence
G-3:   operations and planning
G-4:   supply and transport

In many cases, other sections are indicated as G-5, SJA and so on. However, 1 through 4 are usually standard. There are also "S" subdivisions: S-1, S-2, S-3, S-4, referring to "subordinate" levels of command at the brigade, regimental and battalion levels.

THE FOUR FUNCTIONS OF COMMAND

A breakdown of each of the four basic military command functions follows.

Military Table of Organization

(G-1) MILITARY PERSONNEL

This section deals with military personnel, administering the policies that govern the handling of the soldier as an individual, including general welfare. Its areas of responsibility are:

- morale
- pay
- promotion
- assignments
- replacement if necessary
- burial

(G-2) MILITARY INTELLIGENCE

This section deals with the collection, evaluation and final dissemination of intelligence. It tries to learn the enemy's location, strength and plans. It traces all enemy movements and evaluates them on a minute-to-minute basis. In general, intelligence performs these functions:

- collects data about the enemy
- collects data about the terrain
- collects data about the weather
- collects data about troop movements
- collects data about civilian movements
- carries out psychological warfare
- carries out propaganda, both civilian and military

(G-3) MILITARY OPERATIONS AND PLANNING

This section prepares battle plans and assigns units to carry them out. It develops tactics and directs units to carry them out. It determines:

- overall strategic plan
- tactical (support) plan
- type of assault
- type of defense
- alternate plans
- special forces

The strategic plan and the tactical plan differ in a way that will be explained later. Both, however, are the province of the commander in chief.

(G-4) SUPPLY AND TRANSPORT

This section deals with most of the logistical problems involved in moving troops and supplies. In addition, it handles the construction or restoration of bridges, roads, railways and so on. It is responsible for:

- food and water supplies
- clothing supplies
- arms
- ammunition
- medical supplies
- transport
- gasoline and oil
- portable shelter

To recapitulate, there are four basic staff functions in a military organization:

G-1 administration and personnel
G-2 intelligence: gathering and dissemination
G-3 operations: planning, execution and training
G-4 logistics: supply, transport and medical

These four military functions correspond roughly for discussion here to four main divisions of function in a corporation, designated by the "C":

C-1 administration and personnel
C-2 research and development: new products and marketing data
C-3 operations: production and marketing
C-4 finance, purchasing and transportation

The fourth function appears at first glance to be somewhat different. However, a bit of thought makes the parallels more apparent.

In an army, however unglamorous, supply and transport are extremely critical from the standpoint of execution. Implicit in the overall performance of an army is its primary purpose, its raison d'être: to fight and defeat the enemy. Without matériel, arms and ammunition and without transport (trucks, jeeps, helicopters, boats, etc.), an army cannot adequately fight.

In a corporation, finance is the lifeblood of the organization. Implicit in the overall performance of the corporation is its primary purpose, its raison d'être: to make money for its stockholders. Without finance, a corporation cannot develop its products, manufacture them, market them and carry on its normal business.

Let's review a typical corporate table of organization to see how it is similar to the military command structure:

Corporate Table of Organization

(C-1) CORPORATE ADMINISTRATION AND PERSONNEL

Every corporation must have an administrative division that takes care of the people who work for the company. In some it is called the department of human resources; in others, the personnel department.

This division is involved with workers from the lowest to the highest echelons. The typical personnel division concerns itself with a number of different details:

- morale
- evaluation of performance
- union contracts
- pay scales
- pension plans
- benefits of all kinds
- promotion
- reassignment
- employee welfare

(C-2) CORPORATE RESEARCH AND DEVELOPMENT

Almost every corporation of any importance has its own research and development division. This division continually tries to enhance and improve the products and services provided by the company. R & D includes knowledge about the competition—sales figures, profit figures, inventory assessment, even new improvements and investments the competition is working on.

The *research* part of R & D is usually involved with the deliberate seeking out of information of all kinds—the gathering of all intelligence available to design and make a new product, to investigate the public's interest in it or apathy toward it in the planning stage and to assess marketing data to assure sales. This includes:

- market research
- assessment of competition's sales
- new products research
- engineering
- product security

The *development* part of R & D is usually involved in relating intelligence data to making improvements or in working out bugs that have been discovered in a product. Development is the practical side of R & D; research is the creative side.

(C-3) CORPORATE OPERATIONS: PRODUCTION, MARKETING AND SALES

Every corporation has an operations function that often controls two principal activities of the company: the making of the company's products and the marketing of those items. Overall operations includes all matters of planning and preparing for the manufacture of the company's wares, their fabrication and their promotion and eventual sale.

The *production* division is usually responsible for the manufacture of a product from the raw material provided. In a corporation furnishing a service, the production division is charged with supplying whatever is needed to perform that service. Marketing takes care of advertising and promotion budgets and campaigns, product distribution and the overall process of keeping the company's image before a targeted market.

Marketing is charged with the responsibility to ascertain what products should and can be sold to whom, based on an assessment of market intelligence. Sales is assigned the duty of actually selling the product and reporting back intelligence on customer reaction and satisfaction and what the competition is doing.

(C-4) CORPORATE FINANCE, PURCHASING AND TRANSPORTATION

Every corporation has a division or divisions responsible for finance, purchasing and transportation.

The *finance* function is involved with all aspects of money. Essentially, it is the section of the company devoted to "business." Not only does it seek money for long-term projects and financing, but it also handles the daily payment of bills and salaries and keeps the company financial records. In business, it takes money to make money; finance is involved intimately with money as it comes in and as it goes out.

The *purchasing* function (which may be part of operations) is concerned with the acquisition of material needed for the manufacture of the company's products. It is concerned as well with the purchase of anything else used for the corporation's operations.

The *transportation* section not only moves finished products out to distribution centers or point-of-sale sites, but also sometimes brings in materials required for manufacture.

These three activities are responsible for the following:

- financial stability
- payment of debts
- billing
- collection
- purchasing
- distribution

·   ·   ·

The executive who had his office door painted with the symbol "G-2" was indulging himself in a bit of esoteric humor. He saw marketing research as an important part of intelligence gathering. He was right. Similar techniques are involved in both, although one is a peacetime operation and the other strictly a wartime procedure.

Because a corporate structure is similar to a military structure, as we have seen, techniques that help military commanders win battles should conceivably help corporate commanders win battles in the business world as well.

The question naturally arises: How can winning on a battlefield be equated with selling more vacuum cleaners than the competition?

GEOGRAPHY AND TERRITORY

Battles are usually fought to gain ground, airspace or sealanes that is, physical terrain, geography. It is the mission of a military commander to secure large plots of land and to hold them against counterattack. The target in a military maneuver is usually the acquisition of geographical units of real estate.

Such a geographical unit includes the houses and buildings on it and the people living there. Those are the rules of the war game.

Sales campaigns are fought by corporate entities in a slightly different manner—and yet there is a most important similarity. A salesperson goes out to sell a product to a customer. Usually the corporate salesperson sells not to an individual but to a retailer who in turn sells the product to the customer.

The retailer, or the end-user, then becomes the ultimate "target." In assaulting this target, maneuvers involving shelf space in stores, prominent displays in crowded aisles and the impact of these sales on the consumer all become important in the eventual amount of "territory" the salesperson sells. In sales jargon, the salesperson acquires territory as the number of sales outlets and final sales in the terrain involved is enlarged, almost always at the expense of another product.

The salesperson is one of the "troops," or the "soldier," involved in reaching customers through retailers in the "attack zone." The amount of sales "penetration" indicates the success of the salesperson's attack on the competitor's share of the market. A map of the market share of one or more competitors resembles a map of a battlefield; whoever comes away with the biggest slice of pie wins.

Even assuming the military battlefield analogous to the sales territory, can military tactics and strategies be applied to marketing competition?

Of course they can. And they can be applied to many more areas of typical commerce than the area demarcated by marketing procedures. In the current economic climate, more attention than ever should be paid to military strategies and tactics that can be applied to corporate combat.

"Marketing strategy is the most significant planning challenge of the 1980s, regardless of industry type or size of company," noted a survey by Coopers & Lybrand and Yankelovich, Skelly & White:

> Central to the planning and social trends are the beliefs . . . that most of their businesses will not enjoy unlimited growth in the future, and that economic success will depend primarily on which competitor can capture, hold and increase its share in existing and/or closely related markets.

BASIC TRAINING FOR CORPORATE COMBAT

It's been said that "war brings out the worst in people, and the best in people.

It is true that war brings out the worst in people usually in moments of inaction. It brings out the best in people usually in the heat, terror and rage of combat.

War is a lot of things—but most will agree it is often a case of "hurry up and wait." Of a soldier's days, months and years in the military, only a small fraction is allocated to the execution of combat orders. That execution is based on a number of things, probably the most important of which is training and readiness, which teaches one how to react instantaneously to whatever situation may arise. Military training teaches the principles of combat that must be used in making these important—read "crucial"—responses to problems.

Business is a lot of things, but what it isn't is a lot of waiting. In fact, it is the opposite, even in formerly staid, regulated industries.

Today, the businessperson must operate daily as if the environment is a hostle and wartime situation, with no waiting time available. Competition has stepped up so much that important decisions are necessary from one moment to the next.

A business executive, like a military officer, must be trained, and through an understanding of the principles of war, the executive can better do what is needed when the moment of decision arrives.

The success enjoyed by a military unit is based largely on the application of the principles of war taught to all its members before action. The combat unit that has the ability to react instantly to a situation has learned to do so from careful study and comprehension of these principles. That's why troops drill and march so much— they're always ready for action, no matter what the command may be.

The corporate organization trained in these principles should be able to deal more directly and more effectively—and in the proper mind-set for combat—with any situation that arises. The corporate staff trained in these principles of war should be able to deal more easily and confidently than its competitors with complicated situations in the business world.

THE NINE PRINCIPLES OF WAR

In the instruction of fundamental tactics, the military teaches its officers and troops nine specific principles of war to follow. Over many years of study and practice, these nine principles have been accepted as the basis of military success. They are deceptively simple statements of fundamental precepts for the conduct of warfare that have evolved over thousands of years.

This does not mean that each of these nine principles of war can be applied specifically to a single battle or a single war; all nine principles operate simultaneously in one way or another in concert with the other eight in *any* battle. It is the degree to which each of the nine principles is selected and applied or neglected and ignored that accounts for success or failure.

There is no all-encompassing rule for the application of these principles. They are interrelated and reinforce one another. They can, at times, even contradict one another, depending on the circumstances. The importance of these principles will vary with differing situations.

The nine principles serve as an excellent checklist for analyzing a particular business maneuver that may be used to solve a specific problem.

Here is the list:

- the principle of maneuver
- the principle of the objective
- the principle of the offensive
- the principle of surprise
- the principle of economy of force
- the principle of mass
- the principle of unity of command
- the principle of simplicity
- the principle of security

Maneuver; Objective; Offensive; Surprise; Economy of force; Mass; Unity of command; Simplicity and Security. The initial letters form an odd-sounding acronym by which countless officers and troops learn, often in training and invariably on active duty: MOOSEMUSS. MOOSEMUSS is a constant companion—not only in combat of a military kind but in combat of a corporate kind—for those who win, whether or not they remember or consciously follow the silly acronym.

This book will focus on these nine principles one by one. Then it will explain several other concepts that are necessarily involved in both military and corporate combat: defense, leadership, and morale.

two

MANEUVER

Maneuvers are threats; he who appears most threatening wins.

—ARDANT DU PICQ

In all forms of endeavor, from the simplest acts of daily routine to the ultimate act of survival, the carrying out of a preconceived plan is one of the most stimulating and rewarding accomplishments a human being can experience. Life itself is a long series of maneuvers—requiring planning, mounting and execution—conducted for the purpose of accomplishing ultimate goals.

The key word in the accomplishment of any plan, military or otherwise, is "maneuver." The word, not surprisingly, comes to us from the French, a nation of classic militarists who understand making war every bit as much as they understand making love. Although the term "maneuver" is recognized in all walks of life, including business, it is rooted most firmly in the military world. "Maneuver" is defined as "a military or naval movement," with a further meaning that gives it a bellicose edge: "an action taken to gain a tactical end." Yet the final meaning, which is really its semantic evocation now in common currency, is somewhat different: "an adroit and clever management of affairs often using deception."

In a purely military sense, "maneuver" refers to the movement made by a military tactician in deploying combat power to the most advantageous position possible with respect to the enemy's position, strength and ability. The purpose of any maneuver is threefold:

- to locate the enemy
- to close with the enemy
- to destroy the enemy

An effective maneuver thus contributes materially to the success of any military force in its overall plans by minimizing its vulnerability and maintaining its freedom of action. To be effective, a military maneuver may be an adroit and clever management of strategies and tactics that often employ some deception.

Let's look at a specific military maneuver, remembering that although maneuver is a principle of war, it occurs in conjunction with all the other principles in any particular action.

MILITARY CASE HISTORY

INCHON LANDING (SEPTEMBER 15, 1950)

The Objective

At the close of World War II, an arbitrary borderline between North Korea and South Korea was established to satisfy both American and Russian interests. That imaginary line was the 38th parallel; north of it lay the Democratic People's Republic of Korea (communist and backed by the Russians) and south of it the Republic of Korea (capitalist and backed by the Americans).

Some five years later, on June 25, 1950, the North Koreans crossed the 38th parallel and mounted a strong attack on South Korea. In three days Seoul, the capital of South Korea, fell. Inchon was then taken and the coastline secured. The South Koreans fled to Pusan in the southeasternmost part of Korea and threw up a perimeter of defense around the city. It was a do-or-die stand.

The United Nations met and, with the Russians boycotting the session, decided to resist the invasion of the North Koreans. Command of United Nations forces was given to General Douglas MacArthur, a hero of the Pacific campaign of World War II. The UN objective was to repel the invaders and to reestablish the 38th parallel as the border between the two Koreas.

MacArthur took one look at the map and enunciated the objective:

> The history of war proves that nine times out of ten times an army has been destroyed because its supply lines have been cut off. Everything the Red Army shoots, and all the additional replenishment he needs, comes from Seoul.

The objective would be the capture of Seoul.

But how to do it?

The Strategy

The South Korean troops were confined to a small area to the west and north of Pusan, where they were huddled behind the Pusan perimeter. The full force of the North Korean offense was positioned just outside the Pusan perimeter, exerting pressure continually on the defenders, trying to drive them into the Sea of Japan.

By pushing outward against this strong besieging force, the United Nations troops would be expending their energies in a one-on-one confrontation, with the greatest strength of the enemy poised against them. It was obvious that such a maneuver would be self-defeating.

By trying to mount an attack and penetrating the Pusan lines, the United Nations troops would only put their own forces into immediate jeopardy by exposing them to the full power of the North Korean artillery batteries. Such a maneuver would also be militarily unsatisfactory.

By trying to go around the enemy, that is, by making a flanking attack, or end run, around the Pusan perimeter, the

United Nations forces would invite immediate retaliation by the powerful North Korean forces at the perimeter.

Besides, no matter how effective any ground offense might be, the objective—Seoul—was more than 200 miles northwest of Pusan. What was the point of expending so much energy battling through the North Koreans across miles of countryside and eating up troops and matériel in order to break through to a city at the northernmost extremities of the beleaguered country? For Seoul's position was close to the 38th parallel; by an irony of fate it was at the farthest end of South Korea and it was, at the same time, the position that had to be taken.

And so . . .

MacArthur's strategy was to effect an end run—actually a forward pass—with the receiver in position in the Seoul area. This maneuver would not only deliver Seoul into friendly hands but also cut the North Korean army in two.

Seoul was the target, but it was not there that MacArthur planned his attack. MacArthur chose Inchon, a seaport city within close range of Seoul, as a good primary target. If he could land troops at Inchon, secure a beachhead there and then move eastward to take Seoul, he could make a classic "turning" maneuver against the enemy army and place himself in a position to crush it. And he could do it without the sacrifice involved in the long grinding march through enemy lines to Seoul.

The maneuver would not be solely a land maneuver or solely an air maneuver—it would be a combination land-sea-air maneuver, an amphibious landing in the classic envelopment sense. When he announced his plans to the Pentagon, there was immediate consternation.

General Omar Bradley, chairman of the Joint Chiefs of Staff, who disliked amphibious warfare from the top down, came out strongly against any landing at Inchon—which would be, of course, an amphibious venture.

Bradley cited three specific and overwhelming reasons *not* to land at Inchon:

- Inchon's tides were the second highest in the world—a 29-foot rise and fall of the sea that at times increased to 36 feet! These treacherous tides also moved rapidly; they were capable, according to research, of stranding boats on the mud flats outside Inchon in as little as ten minutes!
- The sea walls in the heart of the city would have to be scaled by landing parties. The North Koreans could easily defend them.
- To top it off, Inchon was guarded by an adjoining island, Wolmi-Do (Korean for "Moontip Island") on which there were heavy fortifications under control of the North Koreans. Moontip Island rose 531 feet above water level, and was the highest point of land in the area. Its guns could lay an intensive and murderous barrage on anyone trying to get past it to Inchon.

One officer in the Pentagon said, "We drew up a list of every conceivable natural and geographic handicap, and Inchon had 'em all."

In Tokyo, the Joint Chiefs of Staff met with MacArthur to try to argue him out of his scheme of maneuvers.

"Inchon is not possible," one of them said.

And that was the very point MacArthur seized on for his argument. "For the enemy commander will reason that no one would be so brash as to make such an attempt," he told them. He then mentioned General James Wolfe at Quebec in 1759, who had succeeded in scaling the cliffs of the city because the French General Louis Joseph de Montcalm had considered the wall impossible to climb. The same was true of Inchon because of its tides and sea walls.

"We shall land at Inchon, and I shall crush them!" MacArthur announced.

The Joint Chiefs caved in.

The maneuver had been outlined. Now it was necessary to make sure that it would succeed. Although a landing at Inchon was definitely an unexpected move, MacArthur could not rely on surprise alone. He had to assure himself in some way that the enemy would not be waiting for him when he landed.

Japan was a country alive with spies and communist sympathizers. Tokyo journalists wryly referred to the Inchon landing plan as "Operation Common Knowledge." North Korea's top master spy was captured one week before the maneuver with top-secret plans for the invasion in his pocket!

Besides that, everyone in Japan could see the massing of the invasion fleet. It was obvious that MacArthur must do something to deceive the enemy into believing the invasion would take place elsewhere than at Inchon.

He did exactly what the dictionary definition of "maneuver" said to do. He managed an adroit and clever affair.

In fact, he planned two diversionary air attacks by the U.S. Air Force—one to take place in the south at Kunsan and another to take place in the north at Chinnampo—at the same moment the landing would be made at Inchon.

While these attacks were in the planning stage, the usual number of people in Japan found out about them and the word went out to the enemy—just as MacArthur intended it should.

The Tactics

The landing went almost as anticipated—at least as anticipated by MacArthur. The diversionary air attacks clobbered Kunsan and Chinnampo, causing the enemy immediate concern for those areas and spreading fear of ground attack in those sites.

Simultaneously came the naval bombardment at Inchon to reduce Moontip Island to rubble. When the army and marines landed on September 15, they made their way into Inchon with little resistance. What resistance materialized was crumpled by the aerial and naval support of the United Nations' ships.

By night the forces were in the middle of Inchon, and by the following night the UN troops were well to the east of Inchon, moving against the North Koreans. Ten days after the first landing, United Nations troops were slashing through the North Korean army which had been rushed to the scene to throw them out. By the end of September, the North Koreans were shattered and the army was fleeing northward with very little semblance of order. All escape routes to the north were in United Nations' hands.

By September 25, Seoul, the objective of the battle, was under attack. It capitulated three days later after a great deal of heavy fighting. On September 29, President Syngman Rhee of South Korea was once more installed in the Korean capital as head of his country.

Comment

The Inchon landing was a classic example of a military maneuver—one that located the enemy, closed with the enemy and routed the enemy. It is true that the United Nations forces did not actually "destroy" the enemy. The North Koreans were routed from Inchon and from Seoul, as they were routed from the rest of South Korea. But they were not pursued and destroyed. They were in fact allowed to retreat, and after they had recuperated, they regrouped, and eventually reengaged in battle—with much more firepower because of the entry into the war of a powerful ally. But that's another story—in chapter 7.

Had they been destroyed immediately, no communist ally except the Soviet Union itself would have been able to join them to return and organize another attack on South Korea.

The psychological element that was such a powerful part of MacArthur's strategic genius—to do it because it was impossible and to do it with just enough deception to make it succeed—was the keystone to the success of the Inchon landing. In the words of Basil Henry Liddell Hart, MacArthur took "the line of least expectation"—and succeeded handsomely in this classic maneuver to beat an enemy of superior numbers, firepower and position.

•   •   •

More recent history—that of the close of the Vietnam War—provides another classic example of the principle of maneuver in action. In this case, the maneuver was not the same type of envelopmental end run that MacArthur engineered, but a very practical example of chess game strategy combined with hardline battle tactics on the part of the commander in charge of the Vietcong.

MILITARY CASE HISTORY

THE BATTLE OF XUAN LOC, VIETNAM (APRIL 1975)

The Objective

In the spring of 1975, the North Vietnamese army (NVA) had pushed back the South Vietnamese army (ARVN) almost to their capital city, Saigon. General Vo Nguyen Giap, top commander of the NVA, hoped that the capture of Saigon would mean the end of resistance against the communist conquest of South Vietnam.

Giap was a "military genius," in the words of one retired U.S. general. "He whipped the French and he gave us fits in 1968 and 1972. He is a master of logistics and communications and his troops are thoroughly disciplined." It was Giap who had done in the French at Dien Bien Phu. He had a penchant for slow, methodical preparation that was not always successful against the highly mobile ARVN tactics, but he seemed to be succeeding in spite of the odds.

Saigon was Giap's primary objective. He knew through intelligence input that the ARVN command, under the direction of General Cao Van Vien, was in the jaws of a nutcracker, politically speaking, with his main support, the United States, applying the pressure. What was needed was stiffer resistance against the NVA. If it was not forthcoming, the United States would withdraw its support and South Vietnam would collapse.

It was known to Giap that Vien had concentrated his main forces at Saigon for a last-ditch defense effort there.

The Strategy

Vien had to protect two key points against attacks by Giap from the north:

- One was the key airport at Bien Hoa, a smaller city about 18 miles to the north and slightly east of Saigon. The highway out of Saigon went north to Bien Hoa and then east toward Xuan Loc, the second key point.
- Xuan Loc was located some 40 miles to the east and slightly north of Saigon. Because of the peculiar terrain through the jungles north of the capital—with the main supply routes for the NVA connecting with the Bien Hoa highway at Xuan Loc—the city was the northern gateway to Saigon.

To take Saigon, Giap had to strike at Xuan Loc, capture the highway, and from there move to Bien Hoa. After that he could move into Saigon along the Bien Hoa-Saigon highway. To forestall this, Vien had concentrated his field troops at Xuan Loc, with an entire division used to resist the assaults of the enemy moving down the highway into Xuan Loc.

The Tactics

Giap moved a heavy contingent of troops into action and engaged Vien's forces at Xuan Loc. A decisive battle ensued, with the outcome not long in doubt. The pressure of the NVA from the north forced Vien to send out an armored regiment to reinforce the weakening ARVN position at Xuan Loc. Despite the added ARVNs, Giap managed a double envelopment maneuver of Xuan Loc, cutting off the ARVN troops in the city.

Now Giap could move on the Xuan Loc-Bien Hoa highway, massing his troops in a swarm that overran the plantations between the two cities, simply ignoring Vien's forces trapped at Xuan Loc. But Vien had a counterplay. He moved some of his reserves out of Saigon in a desperate move to cut Giap's route to the airport and push the NVA back.

Four new NVA divisions moved southwest onto the captured highway that led toward Bien Hoa, where the main Saigon airport was located. They pushed back Vien's troops in a holding action. Meanwhile, Giap wheeled his guns into position in the fields north of the highway and bombarded the airport.

For fear that the NVAs might take the airport, Vien had his forces blow up 300 tons of bombs and ammunition at the airstrip. The airport was put out of operation, and Giap's forces took charge of the entire area. By now, Vien's reserves from Saigon were being systematically chewed up in the field, with no support at all possible from aircraft at the closed-down Bien Hoa airport.

With Giap's troops now outnumbering Vien's in the field by about three or four to one—supplied by NVA convoys coming down the highway—it was all over for Saigon. Giap had won the maneuver by chessboard tactics and excellent generalship, making his moves in such a way that he forced Vien into a series of losing moves.

Giap called the maneuver at Saigon "drawing the tiger from the mountain."

Comment

There were many reasons for the ARVN's defeat. Morale had sunk to a new low. Huge amounts of equipment and ammunition had been lost. Saigon had lost enough manpower to preclude ever again being able to handle the enemy.

The bottom line in the ARVN defeat was maneuver. Giap simply outmaneuvered the commanders of the ARVN troops. After the fall of Xuan Loc, it was a matter of waging a fluid campaign of maneuver in and around Saigon, until an opening could be found to take the city. Giap was up to that.

The result was that with the battle of Xuan Loc, the final resistance of the South Vietnamese army melted away and the war was essentially over. The chess game that Giap had worked out in his mind had won him all the men on the board and effectively checkmated Vien.

. . .

Is it possible to apply military concepts to corporate situations in order to gain commercial success in the business world?

The lessons of Inchon and Xuan Loc certainly do have a practical value in analyzing a certain type of corporate battle. Let's take a look now at a particular corporate objective and strategy that successfully used certain concepts of offensive maneuver to gain a spectacular share of a product market.

In this comparison, consider the battlefield for the corporate maneuver to be a diagrammatic representation of a total market, with each of several competing companies "holding" territorial rights to large percentages of the whole. For "Korea" or "South Vietnam," read "100 percent of the market."

CORPORATE CASE HISTORY

HALLMARK VS. AMERICAN GREETINGS CORPORATION

The Objective

For decades, Hallmark was the king of the greeting card business. Almost alone it created the huge existing market for its specialized product. Competitors had entered the market, but none had ever succeeded in equaling Hallmark's success.

But that commanding lead was not to be held indefinitely. One of the minors, a company called American Greetings Corporation, began marketing a much more modern and less traditional type of card than Hallmark. As companies like American Greetings got into the business, Hallmark continued to remain staid and tied to the deeply conservative traditions of the American middle class, its constant companion—and customer—over the years.

Because Hallmark was the king of cards, it was master of the more lucrative trade outlets: department stores, book stores, stationery stores, gift shops, the more exclusive boutiques. Because Hallmark depended on this exclusivity,

American Greetings was able to make inroads into the less exclusive sales outlets: drugstores, supermarkets, grocery stores, discount houses. Hallmark's cards were expensive; American Greetings' were comparatively inexpensive. Hallmark's cards were traditional; American Greetings' tended to be more attention-grabbing and innovative.

American Greetings decided to fight Hallmark directly— to push into Hallmark's exclusive market outlets as hard as it could, and perhaps even displace the giant. The objective: to grab as much of the lucrative greeting card market as it could.

The Strategy

At this point, American Greetings was in essentially the same position as General Douglas MacArthur was before he conceived the Inchon landing. The company knew what it wanted, but it had to determine what maneuver to use to get it. What it had to do was to establish a beachhead—again, much like MacArthur—in the more exclusive outlets that Hallmark had dominated and controlled for so long. Without establishing that beachhead, American Greetings would still be second-rate.

The company had another problem similar to Mac-Arthur's. If it decided to make a move into the more exclusive bigtime, it might lose its base—its own "Pusan perimeter"— and be pushed right out into the void by Hallmark in a counterattack.

First of all, American Greetings knew it had to consolidate its position as number two in the lower quality card stores and discount houses. Consolidation would prevent any surprise move against it in its home base.

But that would not be enough. American Greetings had to do something impressive enough to make its name known to the public. It had to make that Inchon landing, and make it spectacularly.

Its own problem was even tougher than MacArthur's. He knew where the enemy was. American Greetings did not even know quite how to get through the lines and establish itself in the public mind.

Although the maneuver that American Greetings finally came up with did not involve deception, it did involve adroit and clever management. In short, the company came up with a product that established itself in the public eye. It designed and developed not a greeting card that was superior to that of the competition, but, instead, a corollary, or allied, product—a little doll called Strawberry Shortcake.

It is interesting to note that MacArthur chose the "impossible" beachhead—Inchon with its tides, its fortifications and its sea wall. American Greetings also did the "impossible" to make its stand—it developed the little novelty doll outside its familiar territory of greeting cards.

The Strawberry Shortcake doll had a pink bonnet and a sprinkling of polka dots and strawberries. American Greetings licensed this trademark to scores of producers. The doll appeared everywhere and on everything. The company suddenly became well-known—because of Strawberry Shortcake.

The Tactics

Once the breakthrough was established, American Greetings began going after Hallmark on its own turf—much as MacArthur went after the North Koreans by slicing through the army and cutting it off from its base of supply and higher command structure.

American Greetings now targeted the department stores and the expensive boutiques, expanded its advertising budget, purchased television time in a big way and expanded its line to party goods as well as cards and dolls.

As MacArthur went after the enemy in his mop-up, American Greetings diversified and spread out far past its earlier parameters of the greeting card business.

A look at the sales figures shows how American Greetings' "Inchon landing" went. In the 1960s, Hallmark had a good 50 percent of the greeting card market all to itself. In 1984, it had only 37 percent. In the 1960s, American Greetings' percentage was minuscule. In 1984, it had 28 percent of the market! It had not overtaken Hallmark, but it was well on its way.

Comment

When it saw itself being confronted by an aggressive and brash competitor, Hallmark was forced into rethinking its marketing strategy. It began producing lower-priced cards—something unheard of before. It loosened up its traditional middle-class stance to produce a more relaxed "To Mom and Her Husband" and "To Dad and His Wife" cards (for remarrieds) and to add "Western Images" cards (for those residing in the Sunbelt), along with "Merry Kissmoose" cards featuring a good-natured moose blowing a kiss from under the mistletoe (for the light of heart). It even brought out a competitor to Strawberry Shortcake called Shirt Tales, a line of whimsical animal creations living in a hollowed-out tree, wearing Tee-shirts with the tails hanging out. It doubled its advertising budget, expanded its card sales in drugstores and discount houses, and planned expansion into cable television advertising and production, computer software and direct broadcast satellite. Hallmark still lost 17 points of market share, while American greetings rose from nowhere to almost 30 percent.

· · ·

The case history shows how a corporation can successfully apply the elements of maneuver principles to gain a share of the market—through imagination, ingenuity and resourcefulness—at the expense of its competitor.

three

OBJECTIVE

Complete subjugation of the enemy is not essential in every case.

—KARL VON CLAUSEWITZ

The master, or controlling, principle of war, according to the military manual, is the principle of the objective. The reason is obvious. The objective is the end to be obtained through the use of military force. From a strictly military standpoint, the ultimate military objective is the destruction of the enemy's armed forces—and consequently of the enemy's will and ability to fight.

An objective is generally expressed as a "mission" in military parlance. The mission is then expressed as assigned tasks issued to subordinate units under the command of the officer in charge of all the troops. Assigned tasks, or missions, always combine to lead to the decisive attainment of an overall objective of a unit, a command or a nation.

Nevertheless, this rigid principle—ultimately to destroy the enemy's armed forces and to end the enemy's will to fight—must be subject to critical examination and prolonged discussion. It becomes even more puzzling and susceptible to modification if a typical military objective is used in comparison with a typical business objective.

WHAT IS THE REAL BATTLE OBJECTIVE?

Although common military practice is to define "objective" rigorously and to allow no deviation, it becomes difficult in some instances to isolate the *real* objective, even in a familiar war situation. History offers examples galore of military objectives that were not simply to destroy the enemy army and break its will to fight.

Usually the traditional battle objective was, and is, the acquisition of geography or the prevention of someone else's acquisition of your geography—although in some cases this is not true either. It is not particularly true, for example, when the objective of the battle is the opening of a trade route or of an additional source of raw material for commerce.

Military conquest does not always stop at a settlement of geographical boundaries. The movement of peoples or the devastation of an entire community may be consequences of a military action.

In some instances, the devastated community may have absolutely no connection with the ultimate objective in the war. Our more recent wars supply us with a great number of situations in which the devastation and destruction occurred far from the main objective of the army passing over or through.

The Battle for Monte Cassino, in which the "objective" played a crucial part, occurred during the Allied campaign through Italy in World War II. Granted, the ultimate objective of the war was to destroy Adolf Hitler. That meant breaking through into Fortress Europa and pinning the Nazi leader down in his bunker.

On the way there, a lot of real estate was ruined, a lot of lives were lost and a lot of misery was unloosed almost everywhere. Although it was only an obstacle that nature and man had placed between the primary objective—Berlin—and the Allied armies, the Battles for Monte Cassino became known as the fiercest and bitterest struggles for one military objective in recent history.

MILITARY CASE HISTORY

THE FOUR BATTLES OF MONTE CASSINO (JANUARY–MAY 1944)

The Objective

After bitter fighting in North Africa, the battle zone of World War II moved up through Sicily to Italy, struggling up the coast toward Rome and the route to Germany and France. When the Italians surrendered, the Germans took over immediate command of Italy as an occupied country.

By the winter of 1943–44, American and British troops were moving up toward Rome on the western coast of Italy. On the way to Rome, north of Naples, the Germans had anchored the Gustav line for the winter. That line had a key position, a high eminence on which stood an old Benedictine monastery dating from the sixth century.

Although the monastery became the symbol of the Battle of Monte Cassino, it had nothing to do with the formidable obstructions placed by nature in the way of the invading army. "Monte" means "mountain," and Cassino is a mountain—a plateau, more correctly—rising in a sheer wall of 1700 feet from its base. Nestled at the base of this huge escarpment is the town of Cassino, named for the mountain. Through the town runs Route 6 (the old Via Casilina from Roman times), turning abruptly left to wander about a mile or so to the end of the cliff and then once again toward Rome through the pleasant Liri Valley.

Approaching Monte Cassino from the southeast is a flat plain with little protection of any kind on its surface. Toward the Tyrrhenian coast, bypassing Cassino, lies Route 7 (the old Via Appia, or Appian Way), crossing the River Garigliano. The Garigliano is formed by the confluence of the River Liri and the River Rapido, with the Rapido flowing through Cassino.

Obstacles at Cassino became formidable when considered

in relation to a military advance over that area toward the
north.

- First of all, the road crosses the River Rapido. Although
  only 60 feet wide, the Rapido is 9 feet deep—too deep to
  walk across—and each bank is 3 or 4 feet of sheer cliff.
  The current is, as the Italian name warns, "rapid"—8 miles
  an hour.
- Another problem was the town of Cassino itself, which
  was in the hands of the Germans. It was essentially a German outpost, no longer a town in the civilian sense.
- A third difficulty was the high cliff that dominates the
  valley, from which gun emplacements and observation
  posts of all kinds could be set up.
- The monastery itself was thought to be used at that time by
  the Germans for gun emplacements and observation posts.

The Strategy (First Battle)

Under the direction of General Mark Clark, the Allies
planned a three-pronged assault to take Cassino. On January
17, 1944, the British Tenth Corps would cross the Garigliano
and turn inward to threaten the approaches to the Liri Valley
west and north of Cassino. Three days later, the American
Second Corps would cross the Rapido south of Cassino and
break into the Liri Valley. On that same day, January 20, the
Free French Expeditionary Forces would move through the
mountains on the right and close around to meet the British
from the left in a double envelopment maneuver. The heights
were much more easily scaled on the far right—to the east—
than in the center of the town.

That was the "one" in a "one-two" punch. The "two"
punch included a surprise for the enemy: a strictly classic
beachhead landing of flanking envelopment, an end run
landing on Anzio beach 35 miles south of Rome and northwest of Cassino. Anzio was the trump. The other measures
were incorporated to fool the Germans and engage them in a
feint to distract them from the main punch at Anzio.

The Tactics (First Battle)

The British on the left managed to cross the Garigliano, but were met there by four German reserve divisions. On the right, the Free French made good progress in their envelopment maneuver, but were forced back as they reached the flat of the mesa. They could not get to the center. In the center, the Americans had trouble crossing the Rapido south of Cassino; one division was thrown back. A second, in conjunction with the French, made an envelopment movement up toward the monastery, but was driven back by a strong German counterattack.

At Anzio the Germans were fooled completely. Field Marshal Albert Kesselring had moved two panzer divisions from the Anzio area two days before the Anzio landings to support the contemplated attack at Cassino. Nevertheless, the Americans who had made the landing were unaware of this and spent their time consolidating the position in an area 7 miles deep and 15 miles wide, preparing for an advance on January 30.

By then the Germans were back in force at Anzio after having beaten off the Allies at Cassino, launching vicious attacks against the beachhead.

Thus ended the First Battle of Cassino in failure for the Allies.

The Strategy (Second Battle)

The plan for the Second Battle of Cassino was in effect a continuation and elaboration of the American attack in the center of the first battle. The idea was to assault Cassino from north and southeast at the same time in an envelopment maneuver—a pincers. Then, with a bridgehead formed on the mountaintop by the Americans, an Indian (British) division would storm the monastery and Monastery Hill, then sweep down the hillside south to Route 6 and take it.

Simultaneously, New Zealanders (British) would move along the railway from Naples to Rome and take the station about three-quarters of a mile south of Cassino, a position fortified by the Germans. If both attacks succeeded, Cassino would be pinched out. The New Zealand division and the U.S. First Armored would break through into the Liri Valley.

But in order to soften up the Germans holding out atop Monte Cassino—and, as some thought, holed up in the monastery—the decision was made to pound the monastery into rubble, if necessary, to prepare for the attack.

The Tactics (Second Battle)

The monastery was attacked and clobbered on February 15. No Germans were stationed in it. However, by the time it was leveled, the Germans immediately moved into the ruins and used it as a fortified position. Allied intelligence had been unable to discover if the monastery *was* fortified or not.

As the battle opened, the New Zealanders succeeded in crossing the Rapido and reached the railway station, where they met fierce resistance and were ousted by the defenders. In the mountains the Gurkhas, Rajputs and Royal Sussex (British) moved along an outcrop called Snakeshead Ridge toward the monastery, but heavy crossfire from every point on the top of the Monte Cassino plateau smashed their assault and drove them back in a bloody retreat.

Thus ended the Second Battle of Cassino on February 18.

The Strategy (Third Battle)

The Third Battle of Cassino was to be an attack from the north by three prongs, each moving along one of the three roads converging on the town and Monastery Hill. New Zealanders would be hitting the bottleneck formed by the end of the town and Monastery Hill. The Indian division would storm up the mountainside. The Americans would be held in reserve.

But this time the Allies decided to soften up the town by bombardment in order to clear it of all Germans holed up there. Four hours of bombing, pounding Cassino to dust, would precede the three-pronged assault. The strategy was to wipe Cassino off the map in order to destroy opposition at that key military position.

The Tactics (Third Battle)

Bad weather delayed the third battle for weeks, with the troops living virtually in mud and water. Some were in snow and ice, unable to avoid the soaking rain and the fog and the bitter cold.

When the weather cleared on the morning of March 15, American and British bombers, some 500 aircraft participating, annihilated Cassino by dropping more than 1000 tons of explosive in four hours. After the aerial bombardment, 600 field guns took over. In the end, Cassino was dust.

The New Zealanders pushed down the road in tanks to fight in the rubble for three days and nights against the resistance of the Germans still holding out in the subterranean honeycomb of tunnels in the ruins. The New Zealanders finally reached Castle Hill. The Indian division got to Hangman's Hill, but they had to abandon it on March 24 after a strong counterattack.

Thus ended the Third Battle of Cassino in total failure to reach the objective.

The Strategy (Fourth Battle)

Now the strategy changed. Frontal assault had failed. Double envelopment had failed. Penetration had failed. This time the plan involved four separate moves.

- The Polish Corps would isolate the Monastery Hill area from the north.
- The British would cross the Rapido to the north of town, isolate it from the west and cut Route 6 in two.
- The French would make a thrust across the Garigliano and move up the River Liri into the Liri Valley.
- The Americans, to the left of the French, would also cross the Garigliano and move northwest along the Auruncian Mountains into the Liri Valley.

But—and this was the crux of the plan—the action was to be screened by an elaborate charade. The idea was to trick the Germans into thinking that the big drive would occur not at Cassino, but at Anzio, where inconclusive fighting had been continuing for weeks.

This ruse was to be carried out in two steps. The first was to move elements of the Eighth Army as reinforcements to the Cassino front from the eastern coast of Italy—and to do it in complete secrecy. The key move was for the British Eighth to isolate the town of Cassino and cut Route 6. And that key move would succeed largely because the Germans did not know that the Eighth Army was in the area.

The second step was to trick the Germans into believing there would be action at Anzio. A U.S. division was sent to the Salerno-Naples area to carry out intensive training in breakout operations. All this would be duly reported to the Germans by Italian friendlies. Embarkation areas were marked out; roads leading to them were signposted with the mapleleaf badge of the Canadian Corps; signal exercises were devised to fool German monitors into believing that two divisions were destined to make the landing; in Naples harbor the British navy practiced assault landings; landing craft were brought into the area; the air forces carried out reconnaissance of the beaches at Civitavecchia to whet the curiosity of the residents.

The Tactics (Fourth Battle)

On May 11–12, one hour before midnight, 2000 Allied guns opened up on the German positions at Cassino. The British and Polish infantry attacks started. The surprise was so complete that the Germans were caught totally unprepared.

The combined weight of the assaults, plus the surprise achieved by moving the British Eighth Army forces into position in secret, overwhelmed the Germans. In two days the weight of sheer numbers began to tell. The German right folded. Suddenly a number of troops—French Goums from Morocco—were moving across the mountains toward the monastery ruins.

In the Liri Valley the Germans gave way slowly. By May 16, the British started their penetration move and cut Route 6 south of the monastery, with the Canadians moving up to pass through.

The Polish attack continued. By the morning of May 18, the town was cleared and the Polish flag was flying over the ruins of the monastery.

Monte Cassino fell on May 18. Within 16 days the Allies captured Rome. Two days after that came the Normandy invasion.

Comment

The four battles of Cassino were among the bloodiest and bitterest in the history of warfare. In an area fewer than 10 miles wide, troops of 12 nations from all over the world fought to the death. They battled streams, snow, mud and torrential rain, as well as each other.

The mountains were honeycombed with caves where guns were hidden behind heavy steel and thick concrete. The town of Cassino was savagely defended by holed-up troops. The banks of the Rapido were mined.

And over it all the Germans watched every move from observation posts on the top of the cliffs, covering all the approaches from the south. Killing any would-be attackers was as easy as swatting flies.

As a defensive position that had to be taken—and was virtually unassailable—Monte Cassino was the classic example. It was an objective that chewed up 59,000 casualties and took four months to storm.

It finally was taken—but at what a terrible cost!

· · ·

Another conquest, just as bloody, occurred in World War II on the other side of the globe, in the South Pacific. The objective was as obvious to the eye as Monte Cassino, but more stark and drab. It was Mount Surabachi on the coral atoll of Iwo Jima. When the U.S. Marines were dispatched to take Iwo Jima, there were more than 20,000 Japanese troops in the 8 square miles of the island, hiding in an extensive communications and living system of underground cells. These chambers were protected from artillery fire by concrete made from the island's tough black volcanic ash.

No cover existed to protect the Americans when they landed on the exposed beaches. The conquest of this ugly island gave the marines one of their toughest problems. When that problem was solved and the island was in U.S. hands, the list of the dead was one of the longest in history.

The marines took Iwo Jima inch by inch, crawling on their stomachs or behind their tanks bogged down in volcanic ash. Rifles and flamethrowers erupted as the troops fought their way from pillbox to foxhole, clambering up the one feature of the island, rocky Mount Surabachi. There, on February 23, 1943, after three days of bloody and furious combat, the marines hoisted the Stars and Stripes—and Joe Rosenthal, a photographer for the Associated Press, took one of World War II's most memorable pictures.

Mount Surabachi is a symbol of objective: an objective that took a total of 26 days to secure, and cost 20,965 American casualties, including 6821 dead.

"The fighting," said General Holland M. "Howling Mad" Smith succinctly, "was the toughest the marines ran across in 168 years."

It was an objective that cost a bitter price, but its purchase was worth it in the long run. From that point on, the island was in U.S. hands, affording airfields for emergency landings for 24,761 B-29 crewmen before the war had ended.

· · ·

Not every battle, obviously, is as classic in its approach to an objective as the Four Battles of Monte Cassino or the Battle of Iwo Jima. Nor are the objectives always quite so clearly delineated as the objective of Monte Cassino. In fact, military combat has been waged for many different kinds of objectives over the centuries. Even military theorists differ on defining the "real" objective of war; most seem to settle on a point somewhere between two wild extremes.

ANNIHILATION OF THE ENEMY

One extreme determines the object of war as the vanquishing of the enemy through the enforcement of unconditional surrender. The other extreme determines the object of war as the vanquishing of the enemy through the manipulation of certain conditions and advantages—in trade, in agriculture or in such esoteric areas as water rights (both navigational and nutritional).

Karl von Clausewitz, the famed nineteenth-century general and military strategist, thought of war as a necessary means of national self-interest. Although he has been quoted as saying that the objective of warfare was to vanquish the enemy, he also expressed several contradictory thoughts that moderate that objective.

Most analysts later picked up this sentence in his treatise on war:

The destruction of the enemy's main forces on the battlefield constitutes the only true aim in war.

This was followed as gospel by many strategists and field officers in the twentieth century.

To be fair to Clausewitz, he also wrote:

It is a very different thing whether we intend to follow up the first blow with a succession of others, until a whole force is destroyed, or whether we mean to content ourselves with a victory to shake the enemy's feeling of security, to convince him of our superiority and to instill in him a feeling of apprehension about the future.

In other words, war should depend on reasonable accommodation.

Clausewitz also wrote the lines printed at the head of this chapter:

Complete subjugation of the enemy is not essential in every case.

Certainly that suggests moderation.

Nevertheless, Clausewitz is still looked upon as the first and foremost proponent of war to the death.

Even today the Russians include "annihilation" as one of their nine fundamental principles of strategy. During the Civil War, General Ulysses S. Grant held a similar opinion. He sent this message to General S. B. Buckner, commander of Fort Donelson, in February 1862:

No terms except an unconditional and immediate surrender can be accepted. I propose to move immediately upon your works.

In World War II, President Franklin D. Roosevelt conveyed the same message to Adolf Hitler.

A BETTER STATE OF PEACE

Not all strategists believe in annihilation or unconditional surrender. Liddell Hart more or less states the current feeling in these words:

The "object" in war is a better state of peace, even if only from your own point of view.

He argued that it was Clausewitz's teachings, and the fact that many twentieth-century generals believed in them, that almost wrecked civilization at the opening of World War II.

To understand the varying degrees of military objectives, it is helpful to trace historical attitudes in warfare. A study of these varying attitudes shows that they are reconcilable in view of the changing situation during combat.

THE OBJECTIVE IN MIND

In the beginning, wars were fought by fairly small groups. In prehistory, most likely one tribe or clan would attack another in an attempt to wrest away a good hunting ground or a good piece of farmland, or perhaps even a nice quiet spot for a village. The objective of the battle itself would be to decide the winner and the loser of the battle. Although there might be casualties, there was usually no attempt to exterminate everyone on the enemy side.

As civilization advanced, wars became skirmishes between various rulers whose political positions made them leaders. For certain political objectives, one state might fight against another state, using a group of professional warriors to force a decision. The losing group would then sue for peace. Diplomats on each side of the war would decide on the division of the spoils. Peace would cause both armies to retire to civilian status.

THE CHESSBOARD ASPECT OF BATTLE

In medieval times, war became the attempt of one army to storm the fortifications of another, and thus to seize the city. Various types of siege and repelling machinery were designed and built to enhance siege tactics and countertactics. The objective to be seized at the time was usually a castle or other fortification. At its capture, the contest would be over.

In the days of chivalry, individual knights frequently represented opposite sides in combat, the decision going to the winner of the hand-to-hand "game." In many instances, the death of one combatant resolved all differences, without endangering the lives of large groups of people on the two opposing sides.

During the later centuries, war became more subtle, but the method of using armies to oppose other armies continued in the old-fashioned way. When it was obvious to one commander that the battle was lost, he sued for peace, and the war was over. It was a chessboard philosophy, a winner-take-all attitude in which the victor won the day by the capitulation of the forces opposing him.

BUILDING UP THE STAKES

Technological advances came into play during the early Renaissance and later in the age of the Industrial Revolution. Gunpowder added a terrible dimension to war, making killing at a distance possible, whereas arrows and lances were sufficient in an earlier era. Guns and cannons added a threat of even greater distance. By the time of Napoleon, war was a complex and bloody endeavor involving thousands.

At this point, the whole purpose of war seemed to change. Now an entire state—a whole country—fought for domination over another state. The winner of a war might live to regret letting the loser survive; the chances were overwhelming that the loser would recoup and come back to win the second time around.

Because the stakes had grown, military commanders and the politicians at the heads of state who hired them began to see war not as a struggle for the advantage of one country over another, but as a desperate endeavor to survive in a hostile world. It was at this point that Clausewitz's "total annihilation of the enemy" concept was born.

TERMINATION WITH EXTREME PREJUDICE

By World War I, the concept was strong in the minds of Continental generals such as Marshal Ferdinand Foch. He believed in total annihilation, or *"l'offensive brutale et à outrance"* (savage attack to the bitter end). Bullets, shrapnel and poison gas became the weapons in that war, along with a brand-new weapon, the airplane.

The peace settlement after the war virtually annihilated the German nation and cut up a great deal of Russia and Germany into independent states. The result of the uneven settlement of the spoils after World War I was the rise of Adolf Hitler. The strategists who had viewed annihilation as the end in war gave birth to yet another generation of strategists with the same idea in mind. Hitler vowed to consolidate all Europe under his leadership, annihilating all those who had sought to humiliate Germany.

TOWARD A "REASONABLE ACCOMMODATION"

World War II ended with the suicide of Hitler and the imprisonment or the execution of most of the wartime leaders of the German nation through the Nuremberg trials. All-out annihilation eventually might have led once again to *another* total encounter to the death.

But the positions of the antagonists shifted, and new superpowers assumed world leadership—the United States and Russia. Germany and Japan, who had been the enemies during World War II, were rebuilt through foreign aid and became allies of the United States. However, Russia, a former U.S. ally, became an antagonist in the so-called Cold War that developed following World War II.

Nevertheless, after the "unconditional surrenders" of Germany and Japan, the wars in which major powers engaged were indeed confined to "conditional surrenders," including a long-winded truce drama in Korea and a withdrawal from Vietnam with no decision. The pendulum was beginning to swing from the goal of annihilation back toward one of reasonable accommodation.

OBJECTIVES IN CORPORATE COMBAT

If we assume that marketing strategy looks on territory in the same fashion that military strategy looks on geography, it is interesting to note that the theory of business competition—corporate combat—fluctuates in the same manner as military theory does.

When military objectives were usually simple peace terms with conditions drawn up, business objectives were much more limited than they are today. A small merchant would simply try to outsell the competition, without using cutthroat tactics. There was room for everyone. Marketing strategy was simple and did not involve big numbers.

When the Industrial Revolution came along, business salesmanship, like military technology, escalated precipitously. As in war, the businessperson tried to do in the competition. It was annihilation from beginning to end.

KILLING OFF THE COMPETITION

One example will suffice:

Commodore William Vanderbilt, a nineteenth-century wheeler-dealer—one of the robber barons of that era of American history—believed in the Darwinian theory of the survival of the fittest. When he went into business, he meant to annihilate all the competition.

His favorite tactic was to start up a company, cut prices to undersell the competition and then drive the opposition out of business. He would then raise his own prices to whatever level he chose, for enormous personal profits. He did exactly that when he ran a boat company on the Hudson River and another on Long Island Sound. In each case, he first cut his fares so low that the competition was wiped out. Then Vanderbilt raised his rates—there were no government controls in those days—until the public, which had been pleased with the price war, now screamed for lower rates.

To no avail.

THE TRUST-BUSTERS

The 1890 Sherman Act was passed to disallow such moves by well-heeled entrepreneurs. The Clayton Act in 1914 continued the trend. These were the trust-busting laws that tried to prevent the trusts—large companies with a great deal of money behind them—from joining together to reduce competition and control the market.

In effect, the trust-busting laws were written in order to prevent the establishment of a monopoly on a particular product or service. "Unfair methods of competition in commerce are unlawful," the Sherman Act pointed out, "where the effect . . . may be to substantially lessen competition or tend to create a monopoly in any line of commerce."

In the case of a public utility, such as a city's water company or electric power supplier, the effect of monopoly was mitigated by the presence of elected officials who could and did regulate the price set by the utility and oversaw its growth, expansion and business activities.

Business has not followed the thirst for annihilation the way the military has in this century. A modern merchandiser rarely will adopt an objective of annihilation, even though, like Commodore Vanderbilt's companies, a large well-heeled corporation could easily destroy any small company to drive it out of business in order to control prices.

What prevents such slugfests are the antitrust laws just explained. Even without them, it would be unlikely that a corporate entity would want to sweep the field free of any opposition product or service. Such a company would spread itself too thin over the market, become completely quiescent because of its commanding position and be an ideal target for any clever and resourceful competitor to come along and blow it out of the water.

A PIECE OF THE MARKETPLACE

Most companies today follow Liddell Hart's doctrine that "the object in war is a better state of peace." In other words, when a company enters into corporate combat on a marketing level and tries to take over part of the marketplace from an established competitor, the objective is usually not to annihilate but simply to attain that "better state of peace."

What Company B, in going up against Company A, wants is to attain a certain substantial and profitable share of the product market. As Liddell Hart puts it:

> When a government appreciates that the enemy has that military superiority, either in general or in a particular theater, it may wisely enjoin a strategy of limited aim.

THE PRINCIPLE OF LIMITED AIM

"Limited aim" is the key phrase here. It was limited aim that pre-vented the Korean War from escalating into a worldwide problem. Limited aim kept Vietnam from becoming a nuclear war. In corporate combat, limited aim helps any company to find itself a niche in the market in which its own natural edge and superiority give it a good advantage—enough at least to make other firms think twice about coming in to attack it.

In this fashion, the marketplace is usually occupied by several com-panies, all practicing a kind of symbiotic existence. Each is safe and sound in its own preconceived and precarved niche. If peace van-ishes, it is usually because one of the competitors has failed to main-tain its product quality, because the entire market is changing through shifts in conditions or because a new competitor has appeared with a brand-new idea and concept that marks a *better* product.

In strategy, every military operation ever planned must be directed toward a clearly defined, decisive and attainable objective. So must every business objective.

As we have seen, the objective is usually not to annihilate the competitor, but to reduce its share of the market, or freeze its share in order to make inroads into the territory.

In war, the enemy is known from the beginning. In business, the enemy frequently is not known at all, nor even guessed at. In many cases, a corporate entity can choose its own enemy. The market for products and services is usually so extensive that it is filled by dozens of products that enjoy different competitive advantages and disadvan-tages.

THE "GUPPY" STRATEGY

Some competitive corporations are small, others are large. There are three levels of firms that an aggressive corporation can attack:

- small firms
- equal-size firms
- the market leader

By selecting one or more of the smaller competitors as an objective or objectives, a corporate commander may well be able to pummel, upset and gang up on the opposition enough to soften it up for acquisition. This type of objective selection is called "guppy" strategy. In corporate combat, this is usually the easiest and surest way of winning points on the board—or a peace treaty relinquishing territory.

TYPES OF OBTAINABLE OBJECTIVES

By selecting an equal-size competitor as an objective, a corporate commander should be able to ascertain some obvious weakness in the opposition's position. The competitor may not be doing a good marketing job. Or its customers may have finally become disgusted and given up on the product. On the other hand, if the commander feels he is coming into the battle with superior forces at his command, he must simply make sure that the competitor does not have the resources to knock him out during a crucial phase of combat.

If he chooses to take on a battle to secure a leading market share as an objective, the corporate commander must understand that he is taking a high-risk chance. Yet, such strategy can pay off in big profits and an expanding market if the campaign is executed with deftness and precision. For a recent example of a challenger that entered the fray to mark out a dominant share of a market—and simply to overpower the leader already in position—let's take a look at the everpercolating personal computer market. The combatants, of course, were Apple and IBM.

CORPORATE CASE HISTORY

IBM VS. APPLE (1981)

The Objective

In 1981, Apple Company had almost singlehandedly hewed out a dominant share of the market for the personal computer, although Tandy, with its Radio Shack model, and others were defending adequate portions of the field. Nevertheless, Apple was the avowed leader, helped by its major advertising and promotion campaign that had made a high visibility product out of an almost indistinguishable piece of office equipment.

Meanwhile, the leader of the big computer market, International Business Machines, had been eyeing the personal computer market with envy. Almost alone, it had re-created the typewriter business; now it apparently wondered if it might not be able to re-create the personal computer business too.

Its success in entering the "medium-size computer" market—a strange phrase, considering that "medium" at that time meant $65,000 to $275,000 apiece!—had given IBM an itch to compete in the world of end-users rather than the world of corporate corridors.

And yet there were important considerations that had to be faced. With the average price of a personal computer set at about $3500 apiece, as against $65,000 to $275,000 apiece for the medium-size computer, the profit margin would be much smaller. By selling to end-users, IBM would have a gross margin profit of about 55 percent over and against 65 percent and more for the bigger computer systems.

The decision was made and Big Blue, as IBM is known, decided to go for broke in the personal computer business. The object was to move into the field Apple had so carefully and successfully nurtured and to take it over. Typically, IBM wanted the dominant share. A comment by John Imlay, chairman of Management Science America, an industrial independent software producer, became more prophetic than descriptive:

IBM is trying to paint the world blue.

Once the objective was specified, IBM set up an independent unit to design, build and launch the IBM Personal Computer. The unit was called Entry Systems.

The Strategy

The strategy was simplicity itself. Although it would have been more logical to choose an end run tactic, IBM chose instead to go straight for the objective and wage war toe to toe—not a wise tactic actually, but permissible in the case of IBM because of its enormous resources and its previous success in almost all fields it had entered.

The key tactic in IBM's strategy was to copy Apple's successes. IBM's byword seemed to be: "Everything you can do, I can do better." Step by step, Big Blue aped Apple. It set up a retail network alongside Apple's that was almost a carbon copy. It signed a contract with ComputerLand, the largest franchise chain of computer sellers. It copied Apple's dealer support program. It duplicated its customer education techniques and began to set up a training program to prepare for the coming inundation.

But in order to gain time, IBM did not copy Apple, or even its own common practice, in one crucial element of production. Because speed was essential, IBM decided not to write its own software programs but to commission them to other companies to produce. Microsoft won the bid and wrote the operating system for the IBM PC. In another crucial facet of production, IBM went against its own strict rules and commissioned out certain hardware parts, except for final assembly, to subcontractors.

Generally, the crash program was such a successful copying job that Apple's vice president of sales noted:

> IBM is following us around. But as long as we're leading the parade, we don't mind.

The Tactics

Just by getting into the field, IBM stimulated the industry. Many other competitors began to sharpen up for entry into the new market. An entire subindustry was formed—that of writing applications programs for IBM and IBM-type computers. Another subindustry was being generated as well—

companies that built compatible hardware for the IBM Personal Computer.

The new market, which had been moving along quite normally and profitably for those in it, now suddenly began to pick up speed, dynamism and excitement. The public took note. IBM's image of success aroused interest in businesspersons and individuals. If IBM was getting into personal computers, maybe there was more to personal computing than just video games and mailing lists.

Late in 1981, the IBM PC debuted, and the ponderous process of establishing and staffing the projected local IBM service centers throughout the country got under way.

And yet it worked. The field grew by leaps and bounds, with IBM's "brothers" jumping in—Xerox, Exxon, Texas Instruments, DEC and the others. In 1983, there were 2 million PC units on the market—a market that had not existed a few years before. The extrapolation for 1985 was 5.5 million— and beyond that, the possibilities seem unlimited.

Apple stock took a drubbing when the IBM PC was introduced. When IBM penetrated the market, it was an obvious win—a classic capture of the objective. In Big Blue's case, the key element in the victory was its depth of people resources, its strategic maneuvers, and its ability to consolidate key positions as it won each with superior power and tactics.

Comment

It is probable that at no time did IBM consider administering a knockout blow to Apple, or to any of the scores of other competitors in the personal computer field. Although IBM's resources were formidable, it did not seize the opportunity to overwhelm Apple in the way Commodore Vanderbilt would have done. IBM might have thought that the market was extensive enough to accommodate everyone, and the Antitrust Division of the Justice Department, even under deregulation, was still ever present.

In its maneuvers, IBM actually gave a tremendous boost to the personal computer field, widening its scope considerably.

Not only was the IBM presence helpful in interesting the public in a gizmo that—with its stick shift video game counterpart—had been a household swear word for some seasons, but it actually created a subindustry of suppliers of hardware and software.

Yet, at the same time, it put tremendous strain on all its competitors. Both the image of IBM's consistent success and its tremendous pool of reserves always waiting to take over in an emergency put fear in the minds of the competition. In this maneuver particularly, Big Blue's presence added an indefinable sense of now-or-never to the marketing battlefield.

Oddly enough, everyone profited—at least for a while before the shakeout. The competition found its wares more courteously treated by the public. Hardware builders found more firms for which to build. Software writers found more outlets. It was not in IBM's interest to go for the jugular. Its objective was essentially a matter of limited aim.

four

OFFENSE

"The 'A' in AV8B stands for 'Attack' and that's what the Marine Corps is all about."

—MARINE GENERAL PAUL X. KELLEY
on accepting the first production
Harrier jet from McDonnell-Douglas, 1983

In virtually every military situation, a commander must take offensive action to attain final success. Only in this manner can he impose his will on the enemy—which is the whole point of combat. The particular purpose of the offensive maneuver is to retain freedom of action of one's own forces and simultaneously to exploit the enemy's weakness.

There are three types of offensive manuever:

· frontal attack
· penetration
· envelopment

Frontal attack might be likened to the attack of a bulldozer blade. The operator pushes a long flat blade directly at the obstruction—read "enemy"—in order to rout it.

Penetration is the attack of a snowplow on a snowbank. The operator pushes a pointed blade directly into the obstruction—read "enemy line"—to split it and move both sides apart to clear it out.

Envelopment is like an end run in football. The maneuver is geared to avoid strong enemy defensive positions by attacking the enemy's flank. Usually smaller diversions are carried out to deceive the enemy in order to force him to concentrate troops in areas other than where the attack is being made.

FRONTAL ATTACK IN BATTLE

Let's take up frontal attack first. A likely outcome of a frontal attack is eventual failure or withdrawal—or possibly stalemate. History is full of examples of failed frontal assaults:

In military strategy, frontal assault is a distinct disadvantage. When the British military strategist Liddell Hart studied 280 military campaigns, he found that only six afforded victories for plans based on frontal assault. In fact, none had originally been planned as frontal assaults, but had been changed of necessity during combat through tactical reverses.

- The Battle of Bunker Hill was an example of a frontal assault by the British that failed utterly to dislodge the American colonists, who later retreated of their own volition. The British were mowed down as they came up the hill, after the American colonist Israel Putnam told his troops: "You are all marksmen—don't one of you fire until you see the whites of their eyes."
- General George Edward Pickett's Charge during the Battle of Gettysburg in the Civil War was another example of a frontal assault that fared badly. Confederate General Robert E. Lee's thrust against numerically greater forces at the top of Cemetery Ridge chewed up hundreds of his Confederate soldiers and forced him to leave the field.
- The Charge of the Light Brigade against superior forces of Russians during the Crimean War was responsible for killing two-thirds of the British attackers. The Battle of Balaklava's famous frontal assault resulted from a misunderstanding of orders, with an English light-cavalry brigade, 670 strong, charging into a Russian position with utter disregard for the hopelessness of their task.

Failed frontal assaults are quick battles that are not fought again and again. But frontal assault can occur also on extended borders of nations involved in continual warfare against one another. For example, World War I was a stalemated war along miles and miles of a stabilized front. Both sides suffered a dreadful number of casualties because of a lack of effective alternatives to the frontal assault.

MILITARY CASE HISTORY

THE IRAN-IRAQ WAR (1980–   )

The Objective

The dispute between Iran and Iraq erupted into war on September 22, 1980, when Iraq, under President Saddam Hussein, invaded Iran for what Hussein thought would be a swift, surgical military exercise, the objective of which was the overthrow of Ayatollah Khomeini's regime.

The reason for the invasion was a continuing argument between the two countries over ownership of the Shatt al Arab waterway that divides the countries near the Gulf of Persia. It was in Iranian hands, but Hussein claimed it as Iraqi territory.

The Strategy

Iraq hoped for quick success because it had an active army larger than Iran's. With 14.5 million people, Iraq claimed to have an army of 500,000 regulars, plus an additional 450,000 in paramilitary units. With its huge population of 42.5 million, Iran had an army of 355,000 regulars, plus 1.65 million in paramilitary units. Thus, on paper, Khomeini's army appeared to have the advantage, but, in the field, Hussein's forces were favored. Iraq also had a six-to-one superiority of warplanes, its air force numbering 300 aircraft. Iraq had support from Russia in the form of Soviet-made T-62 tanks and heavy artillery. The Iranian military, once having shared with Israel the reputation of being one of the best trained, best equipped forces in the Middle East, had seen its combat readiness erode dramatically after the fall of the Shah. The withdrawal of American advisors and technical support and the execution of hundreds of senior officers rendered the Iranian armed forces an ill-led political force with a lot of poorly maintained equipment.

The Tactics

The quick surgical military attack failed to unseat Khomeini and only exacerbated the situation between the two countries. The battle deteriorated into a seesaw war after an initial penetration into Iran, with sporadic attacks—one by Iran, another by Iraq—and brief invasions and retreats.

With a continuing border war the only possibility, Iraq began to build up fortified positions all the way from the marshy plains of Basra in the south to the town of Khanaqin in the shadows of the higher mountains to the north. These fortifications, backed by Soviet tanks and artillery, came to resemble the fortifications of the static trench warfare of World War I, with earthen parapets and bunkers lined with sandbags. Along the front, the Iraqi fortifications extended for at least 10 miles deep into the desert by the border.

This line of firepower became a major objective of Khomeini and his generals. They determined to smash the fortifications and break through into Iraq. Iran had one advantage: a three-to-one superiority in population. Khomeini exploited that fact immediately.

Teenagers—and even some children only nine or ten years old—were dragooned into the army and sent out to fight with little or no training. They were told that they would achieve instant martyrdom and be delivered to eternal paradise if they died for their country.

Khomeini began to hurl huge groups of these innocents against the fortifications, calling them Revolutionary Guards. Along with the youngsters, he added elderly men to bolster the strength of his forces. At four- or five-month intervals, Khomeini repeatedly sent out these "troops" to hurtle themselves against the fortified trenches where the Iraqi soldiers waited for them to come within range to be machine-gunned down.

Comment

From the beginning of this continuous frontal assalt, Iranian casualty figures were staggering. The more forces that came, the more corpses that littered the hot, dusty, dry battlefield. By March 1984, it was estimated that more than 120,000 Iranians had been killed in their suicide charges against the Iraqis.

At this writing, the Iran-Iraq war has became a stalemate. In its dreadful monotony of suicide missions against superior firepower it is unequaled in modern times.

• • •

The Iran-Iraq war is included to indicate the tremendous odds against the success of a deliberate frontal assault along a long line, even with numerical superiority. The odds are always with the defenders, with little chance for the attackers to overwhelm the entire line and seize the positions.

It is therefore important for the corporate commander to understand how difficult frontal attack is, and how frequently it proves to be unsuccessful—as illustrated in the Battle of Bunker Hill, Pickett's Charge and the Charge of the Light Brigade.

CORPORATE CASE HISTORY

THE *DAILY NEWS* VS. THE *POST*

The Objective

The *New York Daily News* had a long history of effective tabloid coverage of the largest city in the United States. It was *the* morning newspaper with the biggest circulation in the country. Even with the demise of many of the city's other newspapers, it continued to maintain top place, even though public taste was changing and its "low-brow" concepts from another era were being questioned by the late seventies.

The *New York Post* was the only afternoon newspaper left alive in the city. In spite of the fact that it was less popular than the *News* and not financially healthy, it had outlasted all the other afternoon papers and was now beginning to increase its circulation. Ownership passed to an aggressive millionaire from another continent who infused it with new vitality.

Although still twice the size of the *Post* in circulation, the *Daily News* was having trouble with its advertisers. They had moved over to the more prestigious publication in the city— the *New York Times*. The *News* needed an infusion of life, maybe even a little needleful of maturity.

It was decided that the *News* should make a concerted attack on the *Post*, compete in the afternoon arena, drive the *Post* to the wall, buy it out and thereby control both a morning and an afternoon newspaper in the city.

The Strategy

The *News*'s publisher decided that he would double the *News* from a morning paper to a morning *and* afternoon paper. The "night" edition, to be called *Tonight*, would still be the *News*, with suitable changes in format and graphics to distinguish it from the morning *News*.

And, of course, the upgrading of the material, which the *News* had been doing in a subtle way, would be continued, so that the afternoon edition would be much more sophisticated and mature—for the home-going commuter and whomever—than the *Post*.

Essentially, the *News* brass was deciding to do what a good military commander knows should *not* be done. The publisher was taking a deliberate chance in straddling the night-side and the dayside. Besides that, the *Post* was similar to the *News*—lots of columns, lots of gossip, lots of boilerplate, lots of crude and raunch.

The *News* bought new columns, hired new columnists, expanded its staff to take care of the projected operation and then launched *Tonight* on August 19, 1980. This was a perfect example of a frontal assault, with no redeeming features. There was no attempt to mount a flanking attack, no attempt to mitigate the suicidal Pickett's Charge syndrome of the action.

The Tactics

For a while, it looked as if *Tonight* would get off the ground without too much trouble. The first copies were snatched up, people read them with interest—but then, slowly, the circulation wore down and the advertisers, who had been given cut rates in order to stimulate business, pulled out and went back to the morning *News* and the evening *Post*.

The *News* poured money into a souped-up advertising and promotion campaign. It altered its editorial policy, trying to out-hype the *Post*, which was a pretty good example of hype to begin with. The *Post* even began a morning edition to compete with the *News!* It was a real fantasyland of improbabilities.

Millions of dollars were poured down the drain on both sides. Within a year the venture was deemed a failure by the *News*. The staff was cut back, the syndicated material was canceled and on August 28, 1981, *Tonight* was no more.

Comment

The *News* had made the classic blunder of trying to compete with the *Post* head-on. First of all, its management had not totally analyzed the market situation. Had it studied the *Post* and its marketplace, it would have found that there wasn't much of a market there at all, that, in fact, the *Post* was doing as well as it could *possibly* do, given the situation.

Incredibly, the *News* management had failed to uncover the obvious flaw in the *Post*'s position. The *Post* was operating on a theory almost as outmoded as that of the *News*. The hyped-up tabloid was a thing of the past; the *Post* was hanging on by its teeth. So, in fact, was the *News*. Who needed another tabloid in the 1980s out of the 1930s—with no redeeming pluses? Sure, the material was being constantly upgraded, constantly punched up with sophistication and glamour, but where was the reading audience?

Gone. Gone to the suburbs. Gone to the television tube. Gone with the wind, forever.

Compounding the error in choosing to imitate and surpass the *Post* was the *News*'s tactical failure to capitalize on its own reputation for hype and sensation as a springboard for a new newspaper.

But the basic error was one of strategy. The corporate commander must remember that the odds are *against* successful battle by frontal assault. The advantage always lies with the army *already in place,* no matter how weak and ineffectual it may seem to be from the outside.

The fact that the *Post's* counterassault—the publication of a morning edition in competition with the *News*'s original strong position—*succeeded* is simply one of those aberrations of fate that drives commanders up the wall. There are no absolutes in battle strategy and tactics. Nevertheless, in any engagement there are odds that must be considered.

PENETRATION IN BATTLE

It is not always sheer numbers, firepower or material superiority that decides the victory in a battle. In envelopment tactics as well as in frontal attack, penetration is a key to military success. The trick is to shape the military forces in such a way that the wedge pierces the hard line of enemy resistance. If such a shape can be effectively formed, it can be used to punch a hole in an opponent's front lines and enable one's troops to pour through, thereby disrupting or destroying the opponent's command, control and communication capabilities.

Let's take a look at an example of this type of maneuver in World War II during the Battle for France in 1940. In its way, it was the ultimate penetration tactic. It was performed with military precision by Erwin Rommel—at the time commander of a Panzer division—the man whose book General George S. Patton read and reread in order to defeat Rommel's shrewd tactics.

MILITARY CASE HISTORY

THE BATTLE FOR FRANCE (1940)

The Objective

The German drive to take France began in May 1940. British troops supporting the French and attempting to relieve the pressure on Belgium and the Netherlands were driven toward the English Channel. There they made their escape at Dunkirk.

The second and final phase of the French campaign started in June, with the French army stretched out along a line along the Somme and the Aisne. Rommel's tanks opened up that line with a penetrating movement that completely overwhelmed the French by its speed and surprise.

The Strategy

Rommel was in charge of a tank division. To prevent tank attacks, the French had blown up the bridges over the Somme River, with the exception of the railroad bridges. The trains were in the hands of the French and were being held in reserve to be used in counterattacks during the fighting. The railroad tracks were laid in such a way that the infantry could not use them to walk along because they would be in an exposed position and would be sitting ducks for the French artillery.

But Rommel knew how to get around those problems.

The Tactics

Instead of bypassing these railroad lines, Rommel seized them, ripped up the steel tracks and wooden ties and used the roadbed as a track for his panzers! The French shellfire bounced off the tank surfaces without inflicting any damage.

In one day Rommel had traveled 8 miles deep into the French lines; in two days he was 20 miles past the line; and on the third day, 30 miles. It was such a deep thrust that it split the French army.

Other German tank divisions poured through the gap. On the fourth day Rommel was at Rouen and the Seine River. There he turned westward and headed for the English Channel, where he was able to cut off the retreat of the left wing of the French army.

Comment

It was an example of well-conceived penetration tactics used by a wily commander who perceived a way to utilize the resources at his command to split the enemy's lines and wreak havoc on its rear.

·   ·   ·

Now let's apply penetration tactics to a corporate situation. Penetration is a different type of maneuver from frontal attack or envelopment in that it depends on critical analysis of available intelligence to determine the enemy's weakest point in the line. This weak point is the so-called seam between the various sections of the army. Penetration also depends on massing tremendous force to attack the seam. We'll see this concept of mass again in a later chapter.

Penetration tactics, which can be used offensively and defensively, require quick followup and immediate occupation of the flanks and rear of the opponent's position. This history of a brilliant corporate marketing maneuver involving penetration is a case in point.

CORPORATE CASE HISTORY

JAY'S VS. PRINGLE'S

The Objective

When Procter & Gamble brought out its new unbreakable, crispy fresh potato chip in 1968, it was the result of nearly ten years of painstaking research and development. Pringle's, the new "perfect" chip, immediately had a big impact on the market, and within seven years had 13 percent of the entire national market. In a business dominated by regional brands, this was a substantial accomplishment putting Pringle's in third place just behind Wise Potato Chips, distributed by Borden, and the number one chip, Frito-Lay, owned by PepsiCo.

Pringle's chips actually were not potato chips per se, but reconstituted potato mash shaped into chip form, and marketed in foil-lined tennis-ball cans. They were neatly stacked and guaranteed to come out firm and tasty and unbroken.

Regional potato chip manufacturers, including Jay's Foods, Inc., in Chicago, found themselves with their backs to the wall as Pringle's began chipping away at their markets. Jay's, which held 80 percent of the Chicago market when Pringle's came in, determined to fight back and retain its portion of that market.

The Strategy

Along with the other Pringle's competitors, Frito-Lay and Wise, Jay's began to analyze the Pringle's chips. The main fault with Pringle's was the fact that it was not a chip at all, but a reconstituted product that was then fixed in shape by cooking.

But there were other faults as well. A number of additives were used to preserve the reconstituted chips in the can, including a lot of chemicals that sounded like a poison gas formula.

Another weakness in the Pringle's juggernaut was Procter & Gamble's reluctance to give price breaks to its retailers. While these inducements are not kickbacks, they do give the retailer a legal incentive to handle a piece of merchandise. With Pringle's the break was from 15 cents to 17 cents on the dollar.

Jay's began a three-pronged penetration campaign:

- to attack Pringle's on its unnaturalness

- to attack Pringle's on the use of preservatives
- to attack Pringle's pricing on the retail level

The Tactics

It was easy enough to point out the most consumer sensitive flaw in Pringle's: that it was really a "dehydrated potato mash," a reconstituted dehydrated potato. To anyone who had been served dehydrated potatoes in the armed forces, that was a definite strike against Pringle's.

A simple listing of the chemicals that were mixed in with the potato mash in order to preserve it in the can was enough to arouse the antipathy of almost anyone interested in food content: mono- and di-glycerides were included, along with butylated hydroxyanisole.

And on the retail level, Jay's continued to give, as it had always given, a 25 cent on the dollar break to its retailers to promote sales as compared to the more stingy Pringle's 15 to 17 cent break.

Pringle's found itself in a rough ground war with Jay's in the Chicago area. Jay's penetration strategy seemed to be working. As hard as it pushed, Pringle's found that it was not making much of a dent in the marketplace. In other areas, Wise, Frito-Lay, and even Laura Scudder, distributed by Pet Milk, were mounting similar attacks against Pringle's for its ersatz composition.

As Pringle's found its product attacked on several different levels, it immediately went into executive session and decided on a counter strategy.

Its researchers had been working on methods of avoiding the use of preservatives, and in June 1978 Procter & Gamble announced that Pringle's was going "natural," and would not use preservatives in the future. However, the chip would still be sold in the same can as before, to prevent breakage in shipment.

In addition, Pringle's branched out with several different "flavors" of chips.

Comment

Strategically, this type of marketing battle plan depends on careful study of the opposition's product and on its ultimate ability to market it. In the case of Jay's vs. Pringle's, Jay's, along with other competitors—both on a national level and on a regional level—discovered the true weak spots in an otherwise strong product.

By concentrating on those weak points, the opposition was able to penetrate Pringle's market, disrupt its marketing plan and effectively block Pringle's from making inroads in many sales regions.

In the end, Jay's prevented Pringle's from making its expected marketing dent in the Chicago area, confining the reconstituted chips to only 5 percent of the Chicago market.

DOUBLE ENVELOPMENT IN BATTLE

Most military strategists consider double envelopment superior to, although more difficult to execute than, single envelopment. There is little doubt that double envelopment is superior to frontal attack or penetration. Although single envelopment has done the trick in many battles, double envelopment has achieved ultimate victory in many well-known situations.

While double envelopment is also called a pincer maneuver, it is somewhat akin to encirclement, but in the military it is usually referred to as double envelopment because of the uneven concentration of forces on the flanks.

An example of encirclement tactics is siege warfare, a type of strangulation in which a defensive position is surrounded and cut off from its supply lines and slowly starved to death. The main problem with such a strategy is that it generally takes more time to bring an encircled enemy to its knees than is acceptable for the pace of modern warfare.

In modern battles, with all the technological improvements providing speed and firepower unheard of in ancient times, double envelopment is an important type of strategic endeavor.

MILITARY CASE HISTORY

THE BATTLE FOR STALINGRAD (1942–43)

The Objective

Stalingrad was the scene of one of the most crucial land battles of World War II, one called the turning point of the entire war by many strategists. Up to the time of Stalingrad's siege in 1942, the German army had never really lost a battle, even though certain clashes had not been completely or overwhelmingly won. After Stalingrad, with its ultimate fate, the German army began to experience many more failures.

Stalingrad was an important symbol for both sides. For Hitler, it was a city named after the leader of the Russian people. Hitler decided he must take it at all costs. For Stalin, the city was important not only for its manufacturing of tractors, tanks and guns, but for its personification of him. The Russian army felt the same necessity to defend Stalingrad and its 500,000 citizens as the German army felt to destroy it.

The city itself was a sprawling affair strung out for 20-odd miles along the eastern bank of the Volga River, a city 3 miles wide at the most. It was ideally situated to serve as a fortress-like stronghold.

There was one important strategic reason for the Germans to take Stalingrad. By holding this gate to the Caucasus region, Hitler could cut the Russians off from their oil fields, which were predominantly located in southwestern Russia.

In 1942, the German army once again started to attack Russia after the Nazis' unsuccessful effort to take Moscow in 1941. This time Stalingrad was the crucial objective. The German army was strung out over a 2000-mile front along the western border of Russia—basically a dangerous situation, but one aggravated even more by the Stalingrad salient, a bulge that extended over from the line to contain Stalingrad. This was a corridor that almost invited Russian attacks along its flanks. Yet Hitler allowed the salient to remain.

The Strategy

Overall strategy for the Battle of Stalingrad was carried out by two high officers who were never in the action. Both were impressive personalities, each typical of the country he represented.

For Germany, Foeder von Bock was an old-fashioned Junker officer who believed in aristocracy and the caste system. He wore a monocle and looked every inch the prototype.

On the Russian side, Gregori Zhukov, formerly a peasant from the fields, commanded the troops. He had risen through the ranks to a top spot in the army. He had that broad face of the typical Russian peasant and was as stubborn as he looked.

The German strategy was to isolate Stalingrad by cutting off its access to the Black Sea and destroying its supply and communication lines with Moscow. Then the Germans could take the city and command the entire southwest corner of Russia.

The Tactics (Phase One)

Technically, the first phase of the battle was a siege. It opened on September 15, 1942, when the Germans finally managed to break through the tightly defended outer rim of the city and penetrate into the center. Finally they broke into the factory district and seized control of the "Iron Heights"—the slang term for the area—but two days later the Russians repulsed them.

Reinforcements arrived from Germany in October, with tanks and bomber aircraft, and the Germans began methodically pulverizing the city in an effort to smash it into submission. But the Russians did not leave the city or surrender. It was a stalemate.

The Tactics (Phase Two)

Now began the famous Rattenkrieg—the "rat war." This was a type of street warfare, of building-to-building fighting—

elbow-to-elbow, eye-to-eye, toe-to-toe fighting. The German supply lines were stretched. The weather was threatening to turn cold, with winter fast approaching. Yet Hitler, who read his history and knew what had happened to Napoleon, would not pull out. He poured in almost half a million Germans to take Stalingrad.

Both armies struggled desperately to control the city, but without success. It was a no-win situation.

The Tactics (Phase Three)

On November 19, the Russians began an attack along the Don and Volga Rivers. Three Red armies were involved. By November 22, the Russians had developed a pincers around Stalingrad. The Soviet troops engaged in the double envelopment attacked the stretched and thinly defended supply lines of the German army. Essentially, that meant the German troops inside Stalingrad were cut off from supplies and western bases.

Instead of ordering the army out, Hitler decided to stay. The fighting inside the city continued well into January, but it was really all over for the Nazis, although Hitler would not permit his commander to surrender.

What happened instead was that the Russians, because they could be supplied from the outer lines of the double envelopment began methodically to chop up the German divisions into smaller chunks inside the circle. Through the deadly winter the fighting continued, until on February 2, 1943, the Nazis finally surrendered.

It is estimated that more than 300,000 German troops were lost in the battle inside Stalingrad.

Comment

In spite of its probability of success, the strategy of double envelopment presents problems to commanders who propose to use it. It often demands superior resources and near perfect positioning of troops. In the Battle of Stalingrad, most of these advantages were on the Russian side. They held the ground; they were familiar with the battlefield. They also kept their supply lines open, with the rest of the Russian army at least theoretically ready to back them up.

On the other hand, most of the disadvantages were on the German side. First of all, their supply lines were stretched extremely thin. Second, they were fighting battles all along an enormously stretched-out front line. When Hitler poured in troops from other sectors of the line, Nazi positions were weakened where the troops had left. After the two prongs of the double envelopment linked up, in effect creating an encirclement, the difficulty of supplying the German troops in the trap was a horrendous problem.

ENVELOPMENT IN CORPORATE COMBAT

The same advantages and disadvantages of envelopment experienced in military combat are applicable to envelopment in corporate combat. This type of strategy is designed to threaten the competition's marketing segmentation—that is, its identifiable market groupings and the products associated with those submarkets—one on one along the line in an attempt to break through several places simultaneously.

In other words, envelopment translated into marketing terms involves the continual placement of product against the competitor's product, with added impetus afforded through advertising, promotion and marketing.

Envelopment means using well thought-out market pressure to force the competition into rethinking its product line and ultimately into deciding it is too costly and too hopeless a situation to compete with a superior strangling force.

CORPORATE CASE HISTORY

SEIKO VS. BULOVA, LONGINE ET AL.

The Objective

Through the fifties and sixties, American and Swiss manufacturers had controlled the watch business, with the American Bulova Watch Company and the Swiss Longine's Watch

Company the leaders in the middle-price bracket. Two other American companies—Timex and Texas Instruments—dominated the less expensive market.

In 1969, Seiko Watches, manufactured and marketed by K. Hattori and Company of Japan, determined to compete with the Americans and the Swiss in the lucrative watch market. Seiko—the word is Japanese for "precision"—had come up with a new quartz watch, and felt that it now had a product with which to make an impact on the market.

The Strategy

Seiko reasoned that both Swiss and American watchmakers tended to concentrate on the wrong things when it came to designing their watches and clocks. In a changing world, the Swiss were still going in for the design of the entire watch.

But Seiko believed that a watch was something more than simply an instrument to tell time by. It concentrated not on the overall design of the watch, but on the "aperture"—that is, the *face* of the watch.

A watch was something to show off at a bar, something to start a conversation at a cocktail party, a thing of interest and excitement. With the advent of the quartz design—with few mechanical parts—all the watch could be used to project the proper design.

Seiko chose to project the "instrumentation look," copying the idea from the aircraft and sports car image with its instrument board. The idea would be to try almost everything that could be tried to concentrate on "special functions"—the digital look, the new analog look, the calculator look.

By designing endless variations, Seiko could encircle the American and Swiss watch lines and make penetrations where a certain design might become popular.

The Tactics

The Japanese firm began with an immediate foray into the middle-price range—from $65 to $350—with a large number of models. Seiko even designed some mechanical watches for the diehards. All types of models appeared—digitals, chronographs, miniature calculators. The design became all-important; the watches were conversation pieces at cocktail parties. There was even a calculator watch that had to be operated from a remote switch.

Once the new mid-priced models began to sell, the Japanese flooded the low-priced market with less complicated but effectively designed watches, now competing directly with Timex and Texas Instruments. At the same time, Seiko spread out into the higher-priced market, expanding the price range to go after Bulova and Longine on their highest-priced models.

Comment

By completely enveloping the low- and mid-priced market, Seiko was able to bring pressure on almost every weak point in the competition's lines. With superior design, lower-cost production and outstanding distribution coverage, Seiko reacted quickly to fads and new development.

Seiko now markets more than 400 models of quartz and mechanical watches in the United States and 2300 models worldwide. In less than a decade, it is estimated that Seiko has gained control of almost half the U.S. watch market.

five

SURPRISE

Surprise is worth a thousand soldiers.

—GENERAL MARK W. CLARK

MILITARY CASE HISTORY

THE RAID ON ENTEBBE (JULY 3, 1976)

The Objective

On June 27, 1976, an Air France passenger jet carrying some 250 civilian passengers and 12 crew members—many of them Israelis—took off from Athens on its way to Paris. The flight had originated at Tel Aviv, which accounted for the large number of Israelis aboard.

Shortly after takeoff, a group of seven heavily armed hijackers, who said they were the members of the Popular Front for the Liberation of Palestine, seized the aircraft and its passengers and crew.

They diverted the plane from its Paris destination to Benghazi, Libya, where they forced airport attendants to refuel it for a long flight to Entebbe airport in Uganda, more than 2000 miles away in a line almost directly south into the interior of the African continent.

When it landed at Entebbe airport, Ugandan President Idi Amin appeared with his military advisers—he was also the country's armed forces commander—and placed the airport under military control. He said he would work with the hostages in trying to negotiate with the proper French authorities for their freedom. Yet Amin did nothing but cooperate with the PLO under the guise of negotiation.

The PLO had made a name for itself by mounting terrorist attacks to extort demands against Israel and other nations that were pro-Israel. Amin's nation was not pro-Israel. He pretended total ignorance of the situation involving the PLO terrorists, but opened negotiations on behalf of the terrorists with France and Israel.

The entire contingent of passengers was kept under armed guard. The next day, the hijackers allowed the passengers to leave the plane, but they were held in custody at the airport. Now the guerrillas threatened to blow up the hostages with the plane if their demands were not met.

These demands included the release of 53 Palestinians and pro-Palestinians imprisoned in Israel and several other countries. Unless these prisoners were flown to Entebbe to be exchanged for the hostages, the hijackers would exact "severe and heavy penalties" from the hostages.

The hijackers also condemned France as a tool of United States "imperialism," attacked Israel, denounced the "reactionary" regimes in Egypt and Syria and called for revolutionaries everywhere to unite and free the world. It was typical terrorist rhetoric—but the situation was a grave one. The physical presence of so many hostages in a remote and hostile land made their rescue seem completely unlikely.

Negotiations were conducted by Idi Amin in conjunction with French Ambassador Pierre Renaud. On June 30, three days after the hijacking, 47 of the hostages—women, children and ailing and elderly passengers—were released. The hijackers then announced they would blow up the rest unless all demands were met by July 1, the next day.

On July 1, Israel reversed its traditional policy of refusing to negotiate with hijackers and agreed to negotiate the release of a number of Arab prisoners. The hijackers then released 100 more passengers and extended the deadline for their demands. Nevertheless, Israel was not about to bow to the hijackers. The Israelis considered the seizure of the Air France ship with their own citizens aboard a wanton act of aggression against Israel. They looked on it as a battle situation. As such, it demanded military—or paramilitary—action to free the hostages.

The Strategy

The Israelis decided to work on two levels: both negotiation and action. Four years before, during the 1972 Olympic Games in Munich, Germany, members of an Arab terrorist group calling itself Black September had invaded the Israeli dormitory in the Olympic Village, eventually killing nine members of the Israeli Olympic squad. Five terrorists were killed after the tense and strained negotiations had collapsed.

Israel decided to act immediately, while continuing to negotiate in Uganda. Physical rescue seemed the only viable alternative to capitulation—and with no guarantee against the eventual murder of the remaining hostages—which still numbered 103 after the other passengers had been freed.

Israel also decided to go it alone. But how to rescue so many people under arms in a country so remote from and so hostile to Israel?

Intelligence had the answer: by a paramilitary operation involving commandos. Would it work? If it were carried out in complete secrecy to provide maximum surprise, if it were carried out swiftly before the hijackers could consolidate their control, if it were carried out by means of effective and accurate intelligence estimates, and if it were carried out in complete darkness and with proper deception—yes, it might succeed.

Working quickly with experienced commandos, Israeli intelligence mounted an airborne rescue mission to fly in under the radar screen in three Israeli C-130 Hercules transports. Using intelligence reports covering every aspect of Entebbe airport—and of Uganda generally—Israel planned a mission with the utmost attention to detail. Even the size of the runways and the position of the guards at the airport were calculated in advance and sketched out in painstakingly drawn charts.

The Tactics

On July 3, under cover of darkness, three transports loaded with commandos and a supply of weapons and ammunition took off from Tel Aviv and flew the almost 2000 miles across the Red Sea and hostile African countries to the border of Uganda and eventually to Entebbe airport, located at the southern part of Uganda on the shore of Lake Victoria.

Finding the airport in its unfamiliar locale after several heart-stopping failures, the strike force slipped quietly down to land. Bursting out of the planes, the commandos crossed the airstrip toward the airport in a quietly efficient manner. When they were spotted, the airport guards opened fire on them. Shooting their Uzi automatic pistols and hurling grenades at the defenders, the Israelis rushed the terminal.

Once inside, they cut down the seven hijackers, killing them all. In the melee, in which it was difficult to isolate the hijackers from the Ugandan police, 20 Ugandan soldiers were killed. The Israeli commanding officer was shot to death, along with three of the hostages.

But once the airport was secured, all the remaining hostages were led out to safety. The commandos immediately loaded the hostages onto the planes and took off for the long flight back to Tel Aviv. There was no effective pursuit. The surprise had been too complete.

"This operation will become a legend," said Prime Minister Itzhak Rabin at a special session of the Israeli parliament.

"It is Israel's contribution to the fight against terrorism, a fight that has not yet ended."

Comment

It was the total surprise of the raid on Entebbe airport that paved the way for its brilliant conclusion. Neither the hijackers nor the Ugandan military had thought that the Israelis would come so far to rescue their people. The time—only five days after the initial hijack—was not conducive to mounting an attack of any kind. The place—almost 2000 miles from Israel—was far too remote for staging a traditional rescue attempt. And so it was that the Israelis had done the impossible.

Since it was impossible, it was unexpected. Since it was unexpected, it was a surprise. And because of the speed; the deception; the effective use of intelligence and the darkness, weather and low-flying techniques, it was a total success.

The Entebbe raid succeeded because it was a classic maneuver employing all the elements of surprise.

SURPRISE IN MILITARY STRATEGY

The use of surprise is not new. Along with surprise, several other elements are commonly associated with attack: deception, trickery and timing. But surprise need not be limited to the type of strike force mounted by the Israelis against the PLO hijackers. There are all manner of military surprises.

For example, an unexpected turn of events, the introduction of a new and startlingly deadly weapon, a deliberate ploy that pretends to be one thing but is actually another—all these and many other kinds of intellectual shocks can be used deliberately by the military mind to upset and psych out the enemy.

In business, of course, surprise can prove just as effectively upsetting as in warfare. But in business, as in warfare, the surprise must be accompanied by something else that takes advantage of the surprise to make a decisive movement, to close a trap or to defeat the opposition decisively. Surprise alone is not enough.

MYSTIFICATION, MYSTERY AND MISDIRECTION

"Mystify, mislead, and surprise," Stonewall Jackson once said about the strategy of distraction and deception. Liddell Hart xpounded on the point:

> In the psychological sphere, the same effect is sought by playing upon the fears of, and by deceiving, the opposing command. . . . For to mystify and to mislead constitutes "distraction," while surprise is the essential cause of "dislocation." It is through the "distraction" of the commander's mind that the distraction of his forces follows. The loss of his freedom of action is the sequel to the loss of his freedom of conception.

"Surprise lies at the foundation of all military undertakings without exception," Clausewitz said, "only in very different degrees according to the nature of the undertaking and other circumstances." He pointed out that secrecy and rapidity were two factors involved in the creation of surprise.

Most military strategists state that the general rule of thumb is that battles are won by superior numbers of troops. To make up for any imbalance, *other* stratagems must be employed. Of the other stratagems, the most effective is surprise—along with speed and secrecy.

APPLYING SURPRISE AND TRICKERY TO BUSINESS

The lessons of surprise need not be limited to marketing situations in the unveiling of a new product—there are other facets of surprise to be considered in the corporate battlefield.

Before taking up an interesting "surprise" product that helped change the industry of which it was a part, let's look at the corporate battlefield from a slightly different point of view. So far we have looked at the fighting zone—analogous to a military field—as the share of market for a product or service. All well and good—but there are other dimensions to corporate combat.

One involves the control and domination of a company *itself*. During the recent years of deregulation, the corporate takeover has become dramatic proof of the vital presence of this continual threat to *any* company.

CORPORATE CASE HISTORY

GULF OIL VS. T. BOONE PICKENS JR. (MARCH 1984)

The Objective

In 1901, during the early days of the oil industry, a huge gusher at Spindletop, near Beaumont, Texas, established Gulf Oil as one of the dominant forces in the industry. By the 1970s, Gulf was a recognized titan, one of the "Seven Sisters" of oil firms: Exxon, Mobil, Texaco, SoCal, British Petroleum, Royal Dutch Shell and Gulf.

But Gulf had made a strategic error—it had become dependent on OPEC members Kuwait and Venezuela for supplies. By the late 1970s, Gulf's production had dropped 80 percent. In a frantic attempt to get supplies, the company discovered itself deep in a bribery scandal that displaced four of its top executives.

In 1981, James E. Lee became chairman and CEO of Gulf. In 1982, Lee made a deal to purchase a small company, Cities Service. The buy would provide Gulf with much-needed oil reserves and bolster the company's sagging production. But Cities Service had already been targeted for takeover by an aggressive oil man named T. Boone Pickens, Jr. As head of Mesa Petroleum Company, Pickens had directed a takeover group of arbitragers to buy into Cities Service and control it. These arbitragers were ready to move; it was Lee's strategic offer to buy that put the takeover in check.

Eventually Lee withdrew his offer, as did Pickens. Cities Service went instead to Occidental Petroleum Company. But Gulf was still in trouble.

Pickens had turned to a new target—Gulf itself. In August 1983, Pickens and a group of allied investors purchased a big bloc of Gulf stock. The group then attempted to force Gulf into diverting its oil and gas reserves into a royalty trust. Thwarted in this endeavor, Pickens and his backers moved instead to buy Gulf outright, a plan that involved breaking up the company and selling it off in pieces.

But Gulf struck back. It brought a lawsuit against Pickens's group, charging the group with stock manipulation. A proxy battle ensued.

Gulf's objective was clear: hold off Pickens's seige.

The Strategy

There were three basic strategies that Gulf could pursue:

- It could buy back all the stock that Pickens and his group had picked up.
- It could turn around and attack Mesa just as Pickens had attacked it; that is, it could threaten to buy Mesa.
- It could gather in its bank lines to finance the purchase of some other third company, increasing its own debt so much that Pickens wouldn't *want* to take it over after all.

Before any of these strategies was implemented, Robert O. Anderson, CEO of Atlantic Richfield (Arco), offered Lee $70 a share to buy 100 percent of Gulf's stock—a $13 billion deal. Gulf, now effectively on the auction block, was open to the best bidder. To disuade Pickens, Gulf threatened to buy back all the stock held by Pickens's group.

Although this discouraged a number of his backers, Pickens was still in action. He lined up another Texas moneyman, Carl H. Lindner, chairman of Penn Central Corporation, and was promised $300 million as an investment in Mesa to help in the takeover of Gulf Oil.

The situation was desperate for Gulf. It had made its threat against Pickens; the threat was neutralized. Gulf could not really afford to take over Mesa, and it could not afford to purchase another company. All told, Gulf could no longer avoid a merger. But Lee's doubts as to the financial efficacy of a takeover by Pickens kept him looking for a different deal.

Tactics

On the surface, Gulf made efforts to line up backers in order to carry out strategy number two—to buy Mesa—or strategy number three—to buy a third company and increase corporate debt. Meanwhile, Lee quietly approached six companies. Quick bids were made to Gulf. One of them was from Standard Oil of California, or Socal.

Gulf stock was selling at about $70 a share on March 3, 1984, pushed up largely due to Pickens's interest in the company; it had been at $29.50 in 1983. Socal's bid was for $80 a share. The deal was consummated within hours.

Though no longer an independent company, Gulf had won the battle against Pickens, mostly by the tactical use of surprise.

Comment

Even in so-called defeat, Pickens's group made $650 million on the deal. But what made the Gulf-Socal deal memorable was the quickness of its merger at a time of great stress within Gulf. Had Lee moved less quickly to seal the merger, Pickens might have been able to forestall it. Thus, Lee's tactics were tantamount to a successful implementation of surprise.

But there are many levels of corporate combat, and surprise is equally as important on the marketing level as on the boardroom level. The problem with the use of surprise in merchandising is the fact that fascination at the point of sale—on the front lines of marketing—is usually short-lived. Unless a company has a backup campaign that will exploit the impact of surprise and carry it over into the establishment of a brand-new product line, the surprise has not really served its purpose.

Nevertheless, there are surprises that did become established and remained substantial successes. Let's look at one of them and see what particular elements in its success contributed to its staying power.

CORPORATE CASE HISTORY

THE BEETLE VS. DETROIT (1950s)

The Objective

When the first small-size automobile, or what was later dubbed the compact, the Nash Rambler, appeared after World War II, it was greeted with astonishment, derision and some consumer interest. Designed and produced by the predecessor of American Motors, a firm that was in bad financial trouble, the Nash Rambler helped stave off bankruptcy, at least for a time, for its parent company.

But Detroit did not fully approve of the new size car; its price cut down on the enormous profit margin per unit enjoyed by automobile tycoons and stockholders.

There was also an image problem. The public thought the car was puny and not powerful enough to be an effective competitor on the road. The garage mechanics of America hated it; the compact was difficult to work on because of its small size. After all, American tools were made for big cars, for big nuts and big bolts.

The effect of the compact's surprising size wore off in no time. The compact became something of a nine day's wonder—something that would crawl back into the woodwork and almost disappear.

The unhappy love affair between the American driver and the Nash Rambler was noted in another quarter with some dismay. That quarter was Europe, specifically Germany. Here car makers had come up with a brand-new compact that seemed to satisfy the wants of Germans and other Europeans remarkably well. But the company had hoped to make a killing in America. Rambler's problems gave them pause.

There were several strikes against the German car. First of all, it had been originally planned and named by Adolf Hitler. Second, the Volkswagen Beetle was a rebellious imp—it used no water—it was cooled by air. Third, its designers had decided to put its engine at the rear, close to the drive wheels, in order to give it more traction; that wasn't the American way.

But the Beetle had advantages. It worked in hot weather, cold weather, on all kinds of terrain, and it used very little gasoline. Of course, in the United States, who cared? Gasoline was cheap.

How to market the Beetle? How to neutralize America's prejudice against Der Führer's car, how to break down the public's feeling about an air-cooled engine, how to break down the image of weakness and puniness, how to break down the hungover feeling against the Nash Rambler that had made it a car no one would repair?

The Strategy

Marketing strategists in Germany saw the answer: to tackle that last point and to attack all the other problems head-on. They opened up dozens of service areas, sold a service contract with the car—something unheard of at the time—and promised to maintain and keep in good working condition every Volkswagen Beetle sold.

It was a revolutionary concept that grew out of an astute effort to understand and analyze all the points against small cars current among American drivers. The battle that was to come was a battle to sell the Beetle, to win a good share of the market, but the strategy was based on proper intelligence and analysis of the problem.

The Tactics

The strategic approach worked. When the first Volkswagen Beetles came to America, each was sold with a maintenance contract; each was guaranteed service by scores of Volkswagen garages all over the country, which promised to take care of mechanical problems.

The service plan that accompanied the Beetle was the key to its amazing and continuing success. The *real* innovation was not the Beetle's compactness, air-cooled engine or low fuel consumption, it was the service contract and the personal attention afforded to the car owner!

Comment

In this case, design and innovation were not considered enough by the manufacturers. A brand-new concept in car ownership, along with a brand-new look, took the complacent auto industry by surprise. That concept made the Beetle a lasting thing—not a Hula Hoop or a short-lived Pet Rock.

• • •

Looking at the principle of surprise from a corporate point of view, it is important to consider the elements of secrecy and misdirection. To keep a product or a service—or even the way of marketing a product or service—secret, it is necessary to have good research and development security. In the chapter on security—industrial espionage and so on—we'll deal with the problem in a more multifaceted manner.

There are many parallels between military surprise and corporate surprise. Rumors of a new product coming from a large corporation can cause concern among companies already enjoying prosperity in the manufacture of competitive products. The result is a tightening of the customer base. Spreading deliberate leaks about a new product in order to force the competition to retrench is a tactic used every day in the business world. Even the hint that a strong, well-heeled competitor is coming into the field with a new product may be enough to drive smaller companies to the wall.

Surprise, however, is short-lived; it exists only for the moment, then is dead. To defend against surprise, the corporate commander must have the resources and the strength to fend off the first shock waves and recoup the original position of advantage.

six

ECONOMY OF FORCE

Only he that does great things with small means has made a successful hit.

—KARL VON CLAUSEWITZ

The principle of economy of force is one of the simplest precepts of warfare. The idea is to use available forces in a skillful and prudent manner so that a minimum of combat power is applied at any point, thereby permitting maximum effort to be applied at the point of decision. Stated another way, the principle dictates that a minimum but sufficient amount of combat power must be deployed at points other than the crucial one.

MILITARY CASE HISTORY

THE BATTLE OF BRITAIN (1940–41)

The Objective

In the early part of World War II, when the British quite suddenly and forlornly found themselves standing alone against the Nazi juggernaut after the fall of France, Adolf Hitler was convinced that he had them exactly where he wanted them. It was only a matter of squeezing them until they dropped.

France had fallen to the Germans! Europe with the exception of Great Britain was in their control. Spain and Switzerland were neutral, but Spain's sympathies lay with the Rome-Berlin Axis. And so England was alone.

No island kingdom had ever been conquered by air. Hitler was proud of his Luftwaffe, as proud as Hermann Göring. In aircraft, Germany had almost four times as many planes as England. Göring had 1392 bombers and 1290 fighters. England had a pitiful 704 aircraft, including 620 Spitfires and some ancient Hurricanes.

On July 10, 1940, Hitler unleashed the might of his air force on Britain to pulverize the country until it gave up. Hundreds of thousands of tons of explosives rained down from the skies. Incendiary bombs ruined docks, gas works, rail terminals and the nerve centers of cities. Homes were burned and smashed to rubble. People were blown to bits, burned, crushed under falling debris. Fires raged all night. Small blazes became huge firestorms.

The Battle of Britain had begun.

To stop this aerial onslaught, England had only its courage and one viable weapon—the Royal Air Force. The objective of the RAF was to stop the German Luftwaffe. The disadvantage was the Germans' four-to-one superiority in aircraft—not very good odds even for the people of a fighting nation.

The Strategy

The strategy simply was not to give up. Winston Churchill set the tone. Amid the destruction of his country and his city, London, he strode about puffing on his cigar, holding up two fingers in the famous V-for-victory sign.

The RAF pilots took off in the flimsy Hurricanes and Spitfires to battle the German air force plane by plane. Their objective was to shoot down the bombers and engage the fighter-bombers before the explosives could rain down on London.

The Tactics

The man with the cigar decided to teach "Corporal Hitler" a lesson. On August 25, RAF pilots did the impossible. They flew over Berlin and bombed it—the first of many bombings in the history of the German capital.

Infuriated, Hitler vented his rage on Hermann Göring, who, in turn, took it out on Britain. Since bombing of British airfields during the day was no longer possible because of heavy Luftwaffe losses inflicted by the RAF, he was forced to bomb London at night, with the aim of demoralizing the civilian population of the city. This proved a fundamental strategic error because it relieved the pressure on the RAF just to satisfy Hitler's thirst for vengeance.

The London blitz began on the night of September 7, 1940. Six hundred fighter-bombers escorted by 600 fighter planes dropped tons of bombs on London, which trembled and shook as it burned. But it did not give up. The citizens climbed down into air raid shelters and waited for the bombs to stop.

Four hundred Londoners were left dead that first night; four times as many were badly injured. The raids continued night after night—with only one more daylight raid to come.

The RAF flew up to meet the challengers. In the end, after tons of bombs had been dropped, Hitler finally called off the blitz. England was not, after all, on its knees. After June 1941, there were no more raids on London.

Comment:

Hundreds of RAF fliers had lost their lives defending their island. And yet, because of them, the Battle of Britain had been won by the defenders.

"Never," Winston Churchill intoned, "in the field of human conflict was so much owed by so many to so few."

And that was the accolade a twentieth-century war hero made to the precept of economy of force.

ECONOMY OF FORCE UNDER THE SEA: ANOTHER WAR IN ANOTHER PLACE

While the English were winning the Battle of Britain, Germany was using its own concept of economy of force to win a battle in another area—beneath the sea. Germany had nowhere near the capacity to wage sea war that Britain did. Britain had nine times as much shipping tonnage as Germany. To make up for that lack in maritime strength during World War I, Germany had come up with the U-boat, or submarine, as it came to be called.

By the 1940s, the German submarine was technologically far superior to what it had been in World War I. The *schnorkel*—today called the snorkel—was perfected to allow an undersea craft to recirculate its own air. A sub could stay under for several days. Besides that, the submarine had been streamlined and could do a good 18 knots.

By the outbreak of war, Germany only had about 250 submarines, but they were, unfortunately, astonishingly successful in sinking Allied shipping. As England became cut off from Europe, her only line of supply extended to the west to the United States and Canada. The Atlantic Ocean lay between.

NO ECONOMY OF DESTRUCTION

It was in the Atlantic Ocean that those 250 submarines made their deadliest reckoning. They sank a staggering total of 4770 ships under Allied command—more than 21 million gross tons of shipping.

It was the same concept of economy of force—this time used by the enemy to decimate the Allies.

History is full of people like the brave pilots who defended Britain against the enemy in 1940–41—people who defied the odds and accomplished their missions with a minimum of force. The submariners on either side of the conflict were just as courageous.

GUERRILLA TACTICS

It was a simple matter of historical logic that prompted the success of what we now call guerrilla warfare. At the beginning of history, war was probably guerrilla activity—skirmishes, one-on-one matches, group duels, small encounters. The more complex and complicated the art of warfare grew to become through the middle of the twentieth century, the more like a game with rules and regulations it also became. Without quite being able to understand how it came about, the huge American, Soviet and European war machines began to demonstrate a dangerous vulnerability to an ancient method of attack.

The French discovered this in North Africa in the early years of the nineteenth century. After sending skilled troops to deal with the Barbary pirates who operated off the coast of Algeria, France occupied that country in 1830. The occupation managed to subdue the activity of the pirates, but only because the army was able to control the coastline.

In the Algerian interior the people were unfriendly to the French and defied them openly. Although the French thought they were doing the natives a favor by bringing them civilization, the people continually mounted raids on the occupation establishments along the coast. From the deserts and the mountains, nomadic warriors and peasants would swoop down to attack the French outposts.

Reacting immediately to this type of harassment, the French fought in traditional fashion: by mass maneuver, by using columns of artillery, by traveling with enormous logistic loads of impedimenta, by moving through strange, empty country, which allowed the colonialized Algerian people to hide and make sporadic attacks. The French war machine met only with disaster.

The Algerians were at home in the wilds, and they had excellent mobility. They would gather, attack the columns of soldiers, raid the convoys and burn the French establishments. They would attack the columns on the flanks and at the rear and destroy or steal the expensive equipment. Then they would disappear, melting into the landscape as if they had never been there before the French could adequately respond.

Theirs was a classic type of guerrilla warfare, based on the principle of economy of force.

A similar situation occurred in Southeast Asia when the French began to colonize that area in the nineteenth century. The Indochinese people resisted French political intervention in the same way the Algerians had. The French reacted by progressively occupying the country.

"The pirate is a plant which grows only on certain grounds," wrote Louis Hubert Gonzalve Lyautey, the marshal who served in Indochina and Madagascar before being sent to Algeria and Morocco. "The most efficient method is to render the ground unsuitable to him. . . . There are no pirates in completely organized countries."

It is not difficult to detect a note of irony in Lyautey's statement, made many years before the Americans tried their hand at subduing dissident elements in that same part of the world, in the same country then called Vietnam.

THE UNDERGROUND BATTLEGROUND

World War II saw a new type of guerrilla warfare emerge. While high-profile battles raged between huge armies on both sides, small groups of trained fighters—some trained on the spot—were sent in to mount low-profile attacks on civilians and occupation soldiers supporting the occupying army. There guerrilla fighters were called partisans in the underground war in Europe.

In France particularly, the underground movement proved dramatically effective. From their adventures in North Africa, the French had learned about sabotage and harassment and how to divert with frustratingly apparent ease the scarce manpower resources of the German troops occupying France. It was almost as if a separate war raged between the French Underground and the German army of occupation. In Yugoslavia, the partisan underground flourished as well, with Russian-trained Marxists helping to outwit and disrupt the German occupation troops.

With continual attacks mounted to harass and disturb the German troops as they attempted to keep the country in subjugation, the Western democracies clandestinely supported this special application of the principle of economy of force to demoralize the enemy.

THE POLICY OF "SCORCHED EARTH"

In World War II, Stalin followed the advice of Lyautey to "render the ground unsuitable" to the enemy, although not quite in the sense intended. Here is what Joseph Stalin, as commander in chief of the Russian army, said in his famed "scorched earth" speech on July 3, 1941, to the Russian people:

> In case of a forced retreat of Red Army units, all rolling stock must be evacuated; to the enemy must not be left a single engine, a single

railway car, not a single pound of grain or a gallon of fuel.

Collective farmers must drive off their cattle and turn over their grain to the safekeeping of State authorities for transportation to the rear. All valuable property including nonferrous metals, grain and fuel which cannot be withdrawn, must without fail be destroyed.

In areas occupied by the enemy, guerrilla units, mounted and on foot, must be formed, diversionist groups must be organized to combat enemy troops, to foment guerrilla warfare everywhere, to blow up bridges, roads, damage telephone and telegraph lines and to set fire to forests, stores and transports.

In occupied regions conditions must be made unbearable for the enemy and all his accomplices. They must be hounded and annihilated at every step and all their measures frustrated.

ADVANTAGES AND DISADVANTAGES

One advantage for the side that wages guerrilla warfare is its ability to use an economy of force to a degree impossible in normal warfare.

However, guerrilla warfare has an accompanying built-in disadvantage. The use of such tactics necessitates a high level of motivation among these troops, in order to exert consistent pressure on the enemy forces. Such an esprit de corps may be difficult to inculcate in individuals who work on their own and do not see other people outside their own small group for days at a time; the problem is one of motivation without personal contact.

CORPORATE ECONOMY OF FORCE

As can be seen, the various adaptations of guerrilla tactics are endless. The same is true of guerrilla tactics in corporate combat. Although this type of corporate warfare may be used in isolated instances, it can prove dangerous. However, there are thin lines of procedure over which it is not wise to cross.

BUSINESS GUERRILLA TACTICS ANALYZED

There are all sorts of economy of force tactics that can be used in business today. Although some might properly be discussed under one of the other principles of war, five of them are discussed here because they seem to be what the chief executive officer of a corporation might consider guerrilla tactics.

Let's look at five of these tactics. One has to do with the use of bankruptcy as a weapon; another with personnel raids; the third with takeover tactics; the fourth with buyback blackmail and the fifth uses the courts.

THE BIG BOOM IN BANKRUPTCY

To paraphrase Samuel Johnson's remark about patriotism being the last refuge of scoundrels, bankruptcy was in earlier times the last refuge of a failed businessperson. It was the ultimate degradation of any merchant or entrepreneur. Bankruptcy signaled inadequacy, failure, debasement. It was rare indeed that any person was sufficiently resourceful and lucky enough to come back from bankruptcy and reenter the business world.

Bankruptcy treated a company in the same way that England treated a debtor: It created a situation in which the company could no longer operate; it doomed the company to liquidation of its assets so it could never again operate—exactly as imprisonment in a debtor's prison in England doomed the debtor to an inability to earn money to pay off his debts.

Not only did this policy hurt the company and the owner of the company, but it also hurt all the company's creditors. Rarely did a creditor get anywhere near full payment; a few cents on the dollar was almost considered a gift from the gods.

In the middle of the twentieth century, the bankruptcy laws were loosened up a little, and then altered a great deal. Eventually it became possible for a company in bankruptcy to continue in operation and pay off its debts at the same time. It was an excellent reform; now a creditor might expect 100 percent of each dollar involved in the failing company, if he could wait long enough.

The original idea of bankruptcy stripped the company and its owner of virtually all assets. Many owners had to sell their homes and their properties in order to create liquid assets that could be divided up among the creditors. The reformed bankruptcy laws protect the owner of the company by prohibiting the creditors from taking over certain properties like a home or certain other personal assets.

ABUSES IN THE BANKRUPTCY LAWS

Reform often leads to abuses, and the bankruptcy law reform was no exception. Although some bankruptcies under the reformed laws provided for satisfactory repayment of debts—sometimes 100 cents on the dollar—many of them did not. A company that continued to operate even in bankruptcy courts—the Chapter XI type in the United States—might not really survive all that profitably. Some debts might be paid off; not all were.

Unfortunately, the owner might get off scot-free and wind up living it up in Las Vegas or Miami Beach. This fact was not lost on the companies owed money by the bankrupted.

Another more massive problem surfaced almost immediately. If a huge company went out of business under the bankruptcy laws—if, for example, it did not continue under Chapter XI but simply withdrew from the business world—all employees involved in its pension and profit-sharing plans were suddenly deprived of their funds.

The trade unions immediately sensed that bankruptcy could be used in such an instance as a weapon against their members. Nothing, of course, could prevent a badly run company from going broke and simply closing up shop. This happened even in the profitable society of plenty. Nevertheless, it is obvious that a corporation could go out of business legally and use that fact as a weapon against its employees, against a union with a contract, against a creditor with a huge bill to be paid.

The truth is that bankruptcy in its current form can be used by a corporate chief executive officer as a weapon against the company's own people in voiding out pension funds, against a union with a great deal of money tied up in a variety of benefits and against a creditor exerting heavy pressure against the company. The particular looseness of the statutes as they are construed today makes it easier to use bankruptcy as a high-leverage weapon or tactic that could border on the unfair.

THE BIG BOOM IN HEADHUNTING

In military maneuvers, it is a sensational coup to capture the enemy's general. It happens rarely, but when it does, it is a formidable setback for the captured general's side. That is the reason that chess, invented as a pastime for armchair generals, ends with the checkmate of the king.

In business maneuvers, it is also a coup for a chief executive officer to capture—read "hire away"—a competitor's MVP. That too is a formidable setback for the competition.

Much easier than doing the recruitment oneself is the hiring of a professional body snatcher. An entire business has built up around checkmating the other side's king. It's called headhunting.

Companies that want to raid the opposition pay the headhunter up to one-third of the targeted executive's salary to bring him back alive—which makes the profits for recruiters very high indeed. In fact, in 1983, the demand for executives making $200,000 or more surged 86 percent above the year before. There was also a jump of about one-third for the number of managers wanted in the $100,000 to $200,000 range.

"Last year was our best since 1977," one headhunter said of 1983.

Capturing the opposition king can be the crowning point of the endgame in hard-nosed business combat.

THE GENIAL ART OF HEADHUNTING

Headhunting became a national mania in the 1950s when laggard companies overburdened with corporate fat—those were the men who had made fortunes during World War II while the younger men were away fighting—decided they had to get more able and knowledgeable management leaders into harness to pull the companies out of the doldrums.

When high technology became the byword of success, headhunting became an art form. The ideal was not to steal away a genius, per se, but to get a genius who had already earned his spurs by inventing good company secrets. If he could provide secrets that made one company into a success, he could easily supply new secrets (or even the old ones!) for the right price.

Such was the theory that operated—and still operates—in executive raids.

The truth is that personnel raids can be used exactly as bankruptcy can be used—as a kind of guerrilla tactic to put the competition in a bad position or to help mount an attack on a competitor in a weakened situation.

Although unsavory, personnel raids are an everyday thing in the business world. It's underground warfare played above ground.

THE BIG BOOM IN TAKEOVER TACTICS

Takeover tactics are similar to guerrilla tactics. They can be used for harassment, for eventual absorption or for many other indirect objectives.

It usually works this way. A company goes public, that is, its stock becomes available on the market. The reason for going public is to acquire liquid assets—money—to finance expansion endeavors, to start a new line or product or simply to provide cash for early investors by liquefying the wealth that has been built up on paper on their original and subsequent investments.

Nevertheless, there is a price to pay for floating stock publicly for money.

Suppose that a rival company with a lot of cash on hand, or one that has arranged a substantial line of credit at a bank, wants to take over a target company. The chief executive officer of the rival company buys as much stock in your company as he can. When he gets to 5 percent and then to 10 percent, he is required to file his "intentions" for purchasing the stock with the Securities and Exchange Commission. Usually he says that his purchase of stock is only "for investment"—but at least the target company learns who has been buying up big blocs of stock. Under most state laws, if the rival acquires 51 percent of the stock, he may be able to control enough votes to decide the fate of the target company—to merge it with his, for example. Or he can effectively exert his presence on the board, because he owns a majority of the stock.

Sometimes the company going public holds back 51 percent of the stock to make sure such a takeover cannot be effected. Of course, because state laws vary, companies incorporated in others may need a different percentage. Some of that percentage may be held by small stockholders. The takeover company buys up as many large blocks of stock as possible; then, by controlling close to the majority percentage, the takeover raider moves in on the small, individual stockholders, trying to encourage their support for him and discourage their support for the target company's present management.

By eventually suborning—read "wooing"—some of the old stockholders, or even embracing someone on the board who doesn't like the present management, the takeover company may be able to command a majority and can in effect run the company, or effect a merger.

Takeover is a rough tactic in a rough game of business. Once a takeover is effected, often the executives in the target company are terminated. The only ones who may profit are those few who have golden parachutes—clauses in their contracts that assure them a large amount of money on the condition that the company is taken over by another.

Even golden parachutes have a tendency to get shot down by takeover fighters. The CEO in a company recently acquired in a hostile takeover was supposed to get several million in the event the company was bought. It was. The new owners refused to pay the amount in the golden parachute clause. But the targeted CEO, suspecting his contract might be litigated, had purchased $5 million worth of golden parachute insurance. When the new owners balked on his contract, he simply collected the money from the insurance company.

Often the acquiring company will recognize a golden parachute and pay it off. But if the price is too high, it may refuse and let the executive sue. There's a whole new field of insurance developing today—golden parachute insurance.

THE BIG BOOM IN GREENMAIL

One of the interesting, and rapidly growing, takeover tactics is the "greenmail" businesses, as it has come to be called. Greenmail is a pin-striped cousin to blackmail, with the "green" (green stuff, or money) used as a threat to seek or gain board representation rather than the conventional threat of "black"ening the victim's name. This guerrilla tactic can make a mint for the raider who wants to profit by threatening takeover rather than actually doing it.

It works this way. The raider accumulates a significant percentage of the target company's stock and gathers together a select number of stockholders and threatens to wage a proxy fight for a takeover. Of course the raider may never have intended a takeover at all. The accumulation of the stock is simply a device to force a buyback.

The raider waves his stock in the face of the CEO of the target company, threatening to accumulate more and fight to seize the company. The target CEO knows it will cost a great deal of money to try to ward off this hijacking. But he knows he must do it, or face a hostile takeover that may severely damage the company and most likely ruin management and its ongoing source of wealth-building activity.

His usual counter is to offer to buy back the stock. But the raider won't sell it back—not at the going rate. He adds on a stiff markup. The target CEO must pay that amount or face a fight that will cause everyone misery. Eventually the target CEO gets the money from bank lines or retained earnings or both and pays off the raider. The company is now short on cash and long(er) on debt; the stockholders have been maneuvered, all quite legally, out of a large percentage of their future dividends.

Everybody loses—except the raider. Only a few public companies are relatively immune from greenmail.

Greenmail isn't something that will get one into the finest club, but it may purchase the finest yacht. Nor is it illegal or unethical.

THE LONG LIST OF GREENMAILED COMPANIES

Recent financial history is crowded with the sagas of companies that have paid off in greenmail:

- Warner Communications was greenmailed by Rupert Murdoch, the Australian newspaperman.
- Quaker State Refining was threatened by an operator named Saul Steinberg. The company paid him a handsome profit for his stock.
- Chock Full O'Nuts was cornered by a businessperson named Jerry Finkelstein. He was paid a premium for his stock.
- Texaco was greenmailed by the Bass brothers of Texas. Texaco repurchased a large block of shares.
- St. Regis Corporation was greenmailed by a group under Jimmy Goldsmith. The company bought out the Englishman's shares.
- Gulf Oil was greenmailed too, as we saw in chapter 5. However, in that case the saga turned out a bit differently. The white knight—the good guy who came forward to bail out the target company (at a cost!)—paid off the greenmailers. The white knight was Standard Oil of California (Socal).

PROFILE OF AN ARBITRAGER

White knights, greenmail, sharkproofing, bootstrap takeovers, poison pills, doomsday machines—the language of acquisitions is colorful and sprightly. White knights rescue companies from the clutches of raiders; greenmail is paid to purchase back a kidnapped firm; sharkproofing refers to legal devices to fend off a hostile takeover; bootstrap takeovers are paid for by the acquired company's own money in a rough-and-tumble game; poison pills are methods a company uses to lower its financial value; a doomsday machine is a financial maneuver equivalent to a self-destruct mechanism.

The arbitrager is the person who really makes it all go. Like a pawn in a chess game, the arbitrager doesn't have the graceful moves but supplies the front line of manpower. He is the professional investor who rides along with the head raider—the takeover mastermind—or sometimes with the targets, much like the pilot fish swims along with the shark. The purpose of the arb is to make quick profits from owning heavy positions in a target company's stock.

The arb makes moves to abet or thwart the intended moves of either raider or target. Sometimes he plays both sides of the battleground—making a quick killing and getting out as soon as the final move is made. The arb's final move is, of course, toward the side that puts in the highest bid for the bloc of stock the arbitrager controls. If he guesses wrong, the arbs can lose millions.

THE PROPER USE OF AN INJUNCTION

In the military there is no maneuver similar to a court action. Court action presupposes a community at peace, with the law acting as the peacekeeper. The use of an injunction against a military enemy is an act that can be arranged through a cease-fire, usually negotiated by noncombatants; usually only force of arms can enforce any injunction against a fighting foe.

Lawsuits abound on the corporate battlefield. But these often take years to resolve. The payment of money, by the time it is finally decided and all the appeals steps have been taken, often comes long after most have forgotten the original problem.

Combat presupposes immediacy. Speed in maneuver is essential. Therefore, lawsuits are often out of the question as possible maneuvers in corporate combat. Nevertheless, one kind of weapon the courts use can be helpful to the corporate commander: the injunction.

An injunction is a device whereby one organization forces another organization through the court system to cease and desist from a particular action. In short, an injunction resembles a military action because it is a preventive or preemptive effort.

When International Game Technology, a maker of video games in Reno, Nevada, purchased a video electronics business from Bally Manufacturing Corporation of Chicago in 1978, the contract of sale contained a covenant prohibiting Bally from competing with International until May 1983.

Bally's customers were casino and amusement park concerns. After it had sold a specific part of its business to International, it began to develop new electronic games enabling customers to play draw poker and keno, with the intent to sell the games to the proprietors of gaming casinos and arcades.

International immediately sought a court injunction to stop Bally from developing and marketing these video gambling games in competition with its earlier games, which it had sold to International. The court found that the covenant in the contract did indeed restrict Bally from competing with International until the cutoff date of May 1983.

The injunction effectively denied Bally's presence in the marketing field.

This was war fought on a legal battlefield rather than on a marketing battlefield, at least until May 1983. The corporate commander can consider the injunction —either as a weapon to use or as a weapon to guard against.

· · ·

All the corporate guerrilla tactics discussed in this chapter—bankruptcy, personnel raids, takeovers, greenmail and injunctions—illustrate a few of the techniques of leverage the corporate combatant can exert by understanding the principle of economy of force.

seven

MASS

The principles of war, not merely one principle, can be condensed into a single word—"concentration."

—Basil Henry Liddell Hart

The principle of mass is actually a corollary of the fifth principle, economy of force. Another way to express the principle is to call it the concentration of superior combat power at the point of battle decision. It is important to understand that superior combat power—mass—does not necessarily mean outnumbering the enemy in all areas of the battlefield, but rather mustering sufficient strength at the critical point of battle—the point of decision.

This implication has not been lost on strategists through the ages. "The best strategy is *always to be very strong*, first generally, then at the decisive point," Clausewitz wrote. "There is no more imperative and no simpler law for strategy than to *keep the forces concentrated*." In another context, he said, "*It is impossible to be too strong at the decisive point.*"

The rule which we have been seeking to set forth is, therefore, that all forces which are available and destined for a strategic object should be *simultaneously* applied to it; and this application will be so much the more complete the more everything is compressed into one act and into one movement.

Liddell Hart agreed conclusively with Clausewitz:

> The principles of war, not merely one principle, can be condensed into a single word—"concentration." But for truth this needs to be amplified as the "concentration of strength against weakness." And for any real value it needs to be explained that the concentration of strength against weakness depends on the dispersion of your opponent's strength, which in turn is produced by a distribution of your own that gives the appearance, and partial effect of dispersion. Your dispersion, his dispersion, your concentration—such is the sequence, and each is a sequel. True concentration is the fruit of calculated dispersion.

DETERMINING THE CRITICAL POINT

The key element in using mass in a concentrated fashion is to discern the actual "critical point of battle"—or the place where the decisive action will occur.

Nothing could be more difficult to do. In the heat of actual battle, plans seem to go awry at the same moment. Nevertheless, if a commander is astute enough to judge the point of decision correctly, the commander has the battle almost won.

In chapter 4 we looked at penetration in battle, one of the main types of offense. Mass concentration at the key point of the enemy's weakness is another way of looking at penetration, pushing against the enemy at a critical point with manpower, firepower and mobility.

It is different in one sense. Penetration can occur at any number of points that might not be critical points. In fact, penetration at a special site might be used as a feint to draw the enemy's forces in that direction *away from the critical point of encounter.* The nuances and variations of mass concentration are endless.

The opportunity to mass combat power at the enemy's weakest point does not always present itself to a commander. It usually requires a combination of other principles of war to be able to pull it off. There is no question that the assembly of troops in the next military study was a masterful maneuver combining surprise, secrecy, and knowledge of offensive maneuver.

MILITARY CASE HISTORY

THE BATTLE OF THE CHOSIN RESERVOIR (NOVEMBER 1950)

The Objective

After the successful landing at Inchon, the capture of Seoul and the effective splitting of the North Korean army, United Nations forces quickly moved forward to consolidate positions in North Korea.

Disregarding the threats of China's Foreign Minister Chou En-lai—"The Chinese people will not supinely tolerate seeing their neighbors being savagely invaded by the imperialists"—the "imperialists" continued northward. By October 1, South Korean troops were across the 38th parallel in hot pursuit of retreating North Koreans. On October 7, American troops crossed the parallel. On October 19, the United Nations forces were in control of Pyongyang, the capital of North Korea.

The peacekeeping mission seemed secure. But the North Koreans would not surrender. General Douglas MacArthur shortly discovered why. On October 26, Chinese Communist troops—"People's Volunteers"—suddenly entered the war and attacked South Korean units at the Yalu River. Russian MIGs appeared along the Yalu to hold off U.S. airplanes bombing south of the river.

On November 24, MacArthur announced a "win-the-war" offensive and proceeded to put it into action. He had moved the Eighth Army on a broad front northward in the west and center of the front, with the left at the Yellow Sea and the right anchored at the mountains that ran down the center of Korea. He had moved the X Corps up the eastern half of the peninsula.

There was a division of command all along the mountainous spine of the peninsula, the area 50 miles wide in some places, with communication possible only by radio, air and courier. The placement left an enormous gap, a wide, ripped-apart seam, between the Eighth Army and the X Corps.

Intelligence reports said that about 100,000 Chinese Communists opposed the Eighth Army. With MacArthur's roughly 200,000 troops, he had a two to one edge over the Communists.

That was the way the chessboard of war was set up when the Chinese came into the fight. That was the situation that faced General Lin Piao, commander of the Fourth Field Army, the first of the Chinese commands to cross the Yalu into Korea.

His objective: to split the United Nations command and destroy its units.

The Strategy

Lin was faced by the Eighth Army along the western half of Korea and by the X Corps on the east. Between them he had a natural ally—the rugged mountains that split the line.

Lin's strategy was basic, classic and obvious. He simply had to mass his troops where the UN command was at its weakest—*at the seam*. If he could get his forces there in position to attack, he could split the UN forces in two, turn each army toward the coastlines—the Eighth toward the Yellow Sea, the X Corps toward the Sea of Japan—and chew them up.

But the wily strategy of the Chinese involved far more than a simple appearance in the hills to do battle. For weeks Chinese Communist troops had been moving down into Korea from the Yalu—not dozens, not hundreds, but thousands. MacArthur's intelligence estimated 100,000 communists in Korea; there were really 300,000!

How did they get there and fox U.S. intelligence? They used camouflage of every type to move into place to fight, and no one saw them. Every man, every animal, every piece of equipment was concealed during the day and camouflaged during the night. The troops moved only by dark, from 7 P.M. to 3 A.M. During the day they hid in caves, in mine shafts, in railroad tunnels, under huts—in any kind of shelter they could find. No reconnaissance groups spotted them. They made almost 16 miles a day for 18 days, traveling two hundred eighty-six miles from Manchuria to the combat zone in North Korea.

The Tactics

On November 26, the Chinese army, in full force, attacked both the Eighth Army and the X Corps. The Eighth Army was pushed backward, its right flank almost turned. The X Corps stubbornly held off some of the thrusts but could not maintain a stand. They drew back.

The First Marine Division was flanked and cut off at the Chosin Reservoir. They were flanked to the west to a depth of 35 miles. The road leading from the Chosin Reservoir south was in Chinese hands.

For a while it looked as if the First Marine Division was in a nutcracker from which it could not escape. However, the Chinese had overlooked one key aspect of UN strength—air power.

In a masterful defensive maneuver, the First Marines used whatever air strength they could get and fought their way out of the vise closing on them. Several units were cut to pieces and butchered. However, the main group moved to join the X Corps at Hungnam. That retreat gave rise to Marine General Oliver Smith's memorable statement as commander:

> Gentlemen, we are not retreating. We are merely attacking in another direction.

Smith's movement was a breakout. By December 6, some 10,000 troops and 1000 vehicles "attacked" southward. In the Chosin Reservoir Battle there were 7500 U.S. casualties—and an estimated 35,000 enemy casualties.

The navy evacuated the X Corps in one of its most effective maneuvers.

Said Rear Admiral James Doyle, who carried it out:

They never laid a glove on us.

Comment

If retreating is winning, the UN troops won that round. However, strategically and tactically, there is no question that the Chinese Communists mounted a masterful attack by massing their forces right at the seam of the UN forces—where they were most vulnerable.

The war seesawed after the entry of the Chinese. Seoul fell to the Chinese on January 4 but was back in UN hands by March 14. Soon the UN was again at the 38th parallel. Finally truce talks began, with the war continuing most of the time. It took more than two years of palaver to accomplish a cease-fire, which occurred on July 27, 1953. The Korean War was officially over.

The Chinese Communists were able to beat back the United Nations forces for two critical reasons:

- They were able to exploit the fact that the United Nations forces had split their command along a natural barrier that afforded them a perfect attack target and route.
- They were able to move their forces into the battle zone in secret, without tipping off the United Nations forces in the slightest way as to the enormous numbers of troops involved.

Both these considerations helped make the strategy and tactics of the Chinese a classic study in the use of mass at the critical point of battle. Once a concentration of mass has achieved its purpose, the rupture must be followed up with as much vigor and force as possible to provide position for flanking attacks and then for strangulation and envelopment.

The only reason both United Nations armies were not annihilated in the encounter was their own morale, training and superior air power. Otherwise, they would have been completely wiped out.

MASS OF FORCE IN CORPORATE BATTLES

The principle of concentration of superior combat power at the point of battle decision can be applied to corporate situations with little change in the elements and precepts explained already. The key points in using the principle of mass to win a marketing battle are the same:

• determination of the point of decision of the battle
• study of the competition's strengths and weaknesses
• concentration of mass of force against the weakness

Let's follow through on a case history of the use of this important principle.

CORPORATE CASE HISTORY

SWANSON VS. STOUFFER AND GREEN GIANT

The Objective

Swanson was one of the first and most successful of all frozen food brand names. Owned by Campbell Soup Company, Swanson pioneered the concept of the "TV dinner" in 1953—the frozen food meal that could be heated and eaten in the very package in which it was marketed.

For a number of years, Swanson ruled the roost. The TV dinner became an integral part of American life. The bright aluminum trays—scaled-down versions of the metal trays used by GIs in World War II—became as familiar as bubble-gum wrappers.

But then the American taste slowly changed. Sales of dinners and separate entrées began to drop off. This was particularly apparent in the late 1970s when the work force began to absorb more and more women.

It turned out that working women and single persons wanted to eat a more exotic, better quality type of entree or dinner than the meat-and-potatoes mix Swanson produced. Convenience *and* quality became the bywords.

Stouffer, a brand name owned by Nestlé, and Green Giant, a brand name of Pillsbury's, introduced "gourmet frozen dinners" and immediately produced a succès d'estime. Sales of Swanson's dinners dropped by 23 percent in the five years following 1978. How to get back into the frozen food business? Improve the product? Compete head on?

The Strategy

Campbell helped Swanson by using its own corporate counterpart of military intelligence—market research—to examine the battlefield of the buying public. The numbers and the responses showed that the public now *did* indeed want more interesting and more tasty dishes. The public had become much more sophisticated, much more knowledgeable about the components of foodstuffs and much more demanding in its aesthetic taste as well as its sensory taste.

In examining the competition, Swanson's researchers found that although most of the gourmet dinners were meeting with unqualified success, there were soft spots in the market line, soft spots that could be exploited.

- People were much more diet conscious than ever before.
- Many were leery of the amounts of salt and sodium in prepared foods.
- With microwave ovens, the old-fashioned type of frozen food containers were more difficult to use.
- People were much more quick-food oriented and snack-conscious. Snacks, once anathema to mothers, were now "in."

Swanson's strategy was to go to war by concentrating its efforts on spectacularly upscaling its frozen food dinner line and hitting the competition where it might be weak—in the diet-conscious area, in the low-salt area, in the packaging area and in the bill-of-fare area. Swanson code-named its strategy Project Fix.

The Tactics

Tactically, there were three levels, or lines of attack, involved in Project Fix.

First Level
The first level was to rejuvenate the regular TV dinner line. That included three different parts:

- The kitchen experts began to develop diet-conscious meals that had less salt in them, more meat stock in the gravies and new desserts and sauces.
- The packaging specialists began to repack the dinners in different types of packages, designing brand-new logos to make the dinners look more modern.
- The aluminum tray went out the window, and paper and plastic containers were designed to hold the food. These new trays were designed to make it easier for owners of microwave ovens to heat the food.

Second Level
The second level of Project Fix was to prepare a new line of gourmet meals. The chefs at Campbell made up eight different dinners to start out.

One of them, for example, was breast of chicken parmigiana, with fettuccine Alfredo and Italian green beans—a far cry from chicken legs or hamburger patties. This line was not even called Swanson. It was upscaled to a fancier and more sophisticated brand name: Le Menu®.

Third Level
The third level of Project Fix was to prepare new plates for kids—snack-type food that could be used either as part of a meal or as a snack. Hot dogs, hamburgers and so on were made available.

For adults, Campbell came up with sliced pork tidbits and other variations.

To launch these new upscaled products, Campbell put $14 million into a promotion and advertising budget and led with

Swanson's Project Fix foods—with the new Le Menu line of gourmet frozen dinners.

Comment

Note the paramilitary response adopted by the Project Fix team. First of all, it had made a determination on the point of decision in the marketing battle to come. That decision spotlighted the gourmet frozen food meal as the key point in the fight. Second, it had discovered possible strengths and weaknesses in the competition: strengths in the imagination and exoticism of the competition's menus; weaknesses in the use of sodium as a preservative, the lack of diet-conscious meals and the general packaging which seemed to turn off some younger people. Third, it had decided to concentrate its main strength on the gourmet market and the snack-food market—both segments of the general buying public.

In other words, Project Fix was an exercise in the principle of concentration of superior combat power at the point of battle decision.

Swanson's strategy was a corporate application of the principle of mass.

The competition was weak in diet-conscious and salt-free foods; Swanson immediately pushed hard to improve the quality of its own product in those areas. The competition also had weak packaging; Swanson immediately attacked on that level too. The competition's gaps in the snack-food market provided another point of decision for Swanson to attack.

The brilliant change in the general line of Swanson's dinners and dishes made an immediate hit with the buyers. Not only did the brand-new logo and the revolutionary change in the old GI-type food-tray package help woo new customers, but the diet-conscious menus and the salt-free methods of preservation struck a responsive note.

The strategy and tactics proved dramatically successful. Shortly after the introduction of Le Menu, Campbell Soup Company found that its revenues for the year went up by the substantial sum of $113 million, largely because of its newly introduced gourmet food offerings.

eight

UNITY OF COMMAND

The buck stops here.

—Harry S Truman

THE IMPORTANCE OF UNITY OF COMMAND

In any tactical situation, either of a military nature or of a business nature, there comes a point at which a final decision must be made by a single authority. Only in this manner can coordination and control be assured in order to attain the objective in the manner intended.

In a battle situation, there is no time for lengthy discussion, compromise or nebulous assurances of cooperation. There must be no doubt as to exactly who is in total control of the operation.

In a business situation, as in a military situation, the control of the operation must be clearly understood. Valuable time can be lost by conferences, stroking sessions and other types of parleys. Control of the corporation and its operating units and staff functions must be clearly known.

Benjamin Franklin was only half joking when he remarked to John Hancock during the signing of the Declaration of Independence:

We must indeed all hang together, or, most assuredly, we shall all hang separately.

And Clausewitz noted:

> What a difference there is between the solidity of an army under *one* standard, led into battle under the personal command of *one* general, and that of an *allied army* extended over two hundred and fifty or five hundred miles, or it may be even based upon quite different sides of the theater of war. There we see coherence in the strongest degree, unity most complete; here unity in a very remote degree often only existing in the political view held in common, and in that also in a miserable and insufficient degree, the cohesion of parts mostly very weak, often quite an illusion.

The problem of allies and what to do with them has plagued military commands through the centuries. It was one of the biggest of George Washington's many headaches during the crucial phases of the American Revolution. At first the "army" was simply a group of farmers, woodsmen and merchants gathered together with hunting weapons. Later each unit was the personal command of a separate self-elected commander. By the time the loosely leagued "states" needed a chief of staff, there were so many disparate parts that only a genius or a madman could have put them together into any semblance of a force to contend with.

George Washington was that genius. But even to the end of the war, he lost engagements because of insubordination, outright revolt and even treason. In spite of all those negatives—the kinds of "differences" Clausewitz grumbled over—Washington was able to establish himself at the head of all those separate forces and exert command control over them.

It was not an easy task.

The early American army was fighting a specific battle for a known and understood objective—independence. At the beginning of World War I and World War II, the issues were so large and geographically encompassing that confusion and uncertainty were inevitable in command circles about what to do and where to go.

October 6, 1973 was the day of Yom Kippur, the Jewish Holy Day of Atonement. On that afternoon, Egyptian troops crossed the Suez Canal at five points and attacked Israeli installations on the Sinai peninsula. War raged along a 103-mile front. Simultaneously, Syrian forces hit the Israelis at two points on the Golan Heights. By October 11, the Egyptians, with the aid of new Russian SAM-6 missiles, had established a bridgehead of 60,000 troops in the Sinai.

With the help of U.S. AWACs using "look down" radar spotting techniques, the Israelis plotted the seam between the two Egyptian armies in the desert. With that information in hand, they made their plans to hit the Egyptians right on the seam to split the army in two parts. Denying the Egyptians entry through Mitla pass, the Israelis used that gateway to pour their troops and weapons down onto the canal.

Floating a barge and pontoon bridge across the Suez just north of the Great Bitter Lake, the Israelis counterattacked on October 15, with 20,000 troops and 500 tanks. There they launched a three-pronged attack into Egypt and cut the Suez-Cairo highway before isolating and encircling the city of Suez. The entire Egyptian Third Corps was trapped in the Sinai, ringed by Israeli steel.

The Israelis pushed some 20 to 25 miles into Egypt, within 30 miles of Cairo. The Egyptian army was split in two; neither segment could break out of the jaws of their traps.

The Yom Kippur war was over by October 24.

·   ·   ·

On November 26, 1950, similar strategy and tactics were used on the United Nations forces in Korea by the Chinese Communists, as discussed earlier. The Chinese used the seam between the U.S. Eighth Army and X Corps to drive a deep wedge between the two commands, turning each toward its respective seacoast. As a result, the First Marine Division was trapped at Chosin Reservoir and had to fight its way out to survive.

·   ·   ·

The lesson in these two thumbnail sketches of contemporary battles is that without unity of command, an armed force can function but only far below its capacity. If the overall commander allows the enemy to split a command into two parts, or three, or four, quite probably the isolated command is in trouble. Each part of a severed angleworm may be able to grow into a whole worm; this is not usually possible for a military force cut in two.

This is the functional aspect of unity of command. There is, however, an important corollary—the psychological aspect. A look at this facet of unity of command is more complex and will be taken up in the rest of this chapter.

THE BIG THREE AND THE THREE WAYS TO GO

Consider World War II. Great Britain had been almost entirely isolated by the German and Italian occupation of Western Europe, and Russia was the only power still able to fight the Germans. When America entered the war after Japan's attack on Pearl Harbor, the Russians wanted immediate relief: the so-called second front. That was to be an invasion of Western Europe by Britain and the United States.

Churchill wanted to go by a different route—south to the Mediterranean, and then strike upward in Yugoslavia. Roosevelt was the mediator between Churchill and Stalin. It was eventually decided to go through Africa and up through Italy. Then an invasion of Europe could be accomplished from the west, with the armies moving from the west and the south in concert to close the pincers on Hitler's Berlin.

Compromises never work as well as bold ideas. The Italian campaign bogged down after Rome was taken. A war that should have been ended quickly dragged on and on. Italy was still harboring Germans even after the D-Day invasion of Normandy in June 1944.

Let's take a look at a crucial military situation in which unity of command played a leading role. Although unity of command must be firm and established in any battle, it is noticeable only when it is lacking; unity of command is much less understood in its observation than in its breach. I will approach the subject with an example of a violation of unity of command that almost led to disaster in a crucial battle.

MILITARY CASE HISTORY

THE BATTLE OF THE BULGE (DECEMBER 1944– FEBRUARY 1945)

THE OBJECTIVE

After the Normandy landings in June 1944, the Western Allies under the command of General Dwight D. Eisenhower continued to push across the face of Western Europe toward the Rhine River along a very broad front. Eisenhower was

Supreme Commander of Allied Powers in Europe. Under him were Generals Omar Bradley, George Patton and Bernard L. Montgomery, among others. Although Eisenhower had been given full command of the invasion forces, there was frequent friction between him and Montgomery, who had pleaded for and been refused overall command of the invasion forces and even his own separate command.

Of all these generals, Eisenhower was the most balanced, the most low-profile, the most low key. His very genius at effecting compromise was the reason he had been selected over the other leaders eager for the command.

The opposite of Eisenhower in temperament and methods was Montgomery. Fiery, volatile and in greater need of ego-stroking than anyone else in the invasion forces, Montgomery had made himself a hero in the North African campaign against Rommel years before. And yet it was said of Monty:

> In defense, indomitable; in attack, indefatigable; in victory, insufferable!

Bradley was like Eisenhower—low-key, quiet, thoughtful. His genius was in selecting others for command posts and leading them in combat. He was less flamboyant than most of his associates, but he had his own ideas of strategy and tactics too.

Patton was somewhat akin to Montgomery in temperament—hard-headed, nasty, opinionated, contemptuous of failure. He packed huge pistols at his waist, like a leftover hero from the Wild West. He had been reprimanded for striking a soldier in the face at a hospital in Sicily and had only recently been reinstated to command status. Patton was a "go" person, a pusher, a mover and shaker, a four-letter leader of men.

From the beginning of the invasion there were arguments among these men regarding strategy, tactics and maneuvers. Montgomery wanted to move straight across Europe in a narrow corridor, with a concentrated thrust right at the heart of Hitler's Germany, Berlin the target. His was a penetration maneuver.

Eisenhower disagreed. He wanted to move all the troops along in a massive sweep across a wide front, consolidating positions as they came up, at a much more restrained pace than that envisioned by Montgomery.

Montgomery complained later that his idea, which he thought was better, had not been considered fairly.

> I was unable to persuade the Americans to take the risk—which, in any case, was practically nil. So it was *not* done, and the war went on into 1945—thus increasing our postwar political problems, and tragically wasting a great many valuable young lives.

In Eisenhower's concept, the liberation of Paris was a must. When it occurred, there was spectacular press coverage; it was a media coup of astronomical proportions. Morale was elevated in all the occupied countries of Europe, Russia was elated and the United States savored the saving of a traditional, time-tested friend.

Like Montgomery, Bradley, even in his low-key way, was unhappy with the diversion from Germany to liberate Paris. He had wanted to move quickly toward Germany.

> We needed just two more weeks of gasoline [to reach the Rhine]. . . . Those were my thoughts about Paris. I didn't want to lose those two weeks there, and perhaps we did.

Patton was fuming as usual at the lack of gasoline because so much had been diverted to the liberation of Paris. He sat at the head of his stalled tank columns waiting for refueling, fretting and turning the air around him blue with his characteristic and picturesque locker-room bluster.

The Strategy

By November, the massive Allied line was stretched along the Hurtgen Forest in Germany. The British and Canadians were to the north on the left side of the Allied line; the Americans to the south on the right side of the line. One German town, Aachen, the ancient citadel of Charlemagne, was taken just inside the German borders. It was the first Allied penetration of the country, and it set the stage for the Battle of the Bulge.

For weeks Hitler had been planning a huge counterattack that would send the Allied forces reeling. Intelligence reports brought news to the Führer's bunker in Berlin that there was dissension between the Allied leaders. Probes had also discovered that the 80 miles of the front strung out through the Ardennes Forest were held by five American divisions— three of them battle virgins, untried in combat.

Fortuitously for Hitler, that was the point where the two separate armies joined. The seam of the Allied line lay right in the Ardennes. Hitler laid his plans carefully. The maneuver was a classic one: by massing his strength there and hurling an offensive directly at the seam of the Allied lines and penetrating through to reach the seaport town of Antwerp in Belgium, Hitler could cut the Allied front in two, isolating the Americans to the south and the British and Canadians to the north. That would hamper their unity of command and force the isolated armies to fight separately, sacrificing their combined strengths.

The Tactics

On December 16, Marshall Gunther von Kluge moved his troops through a sudden fog that had descended on the forest, thus preventing the Allies from using air support against the Germans, and what became the Battle of the Bulge was on.

Both Eisenhower and Bradley were puzzled by the move, although Eisenhower immediately moved in armored divisions to help out. Bradley thought that it was only a slight feint to try to forestall Patton's drive in the south.

Montgomery was receiving intelligence from his own scouts. Without consulting Eisenhower, he moved his own divisions to the west back of the Meuse between Liege and Namur, waiting for the Germans to cross the Meuse. Unknown to Eisenhower, he met with Bradley and Patton at Verdun on December 19, and all American troops north of the line Givet-Houffalize-Prum were placed under Montgomery's command. He ordered Patton to move toward Bastogne where the Germans had surrounded the town with a wall of armor.

That was as far as the bulge extended. Suddenly the skies cleared and the Allied air forces intervened. Meanwhile, the Germans had run out of fuel for their tanks. Patton's division punched a hole in the wall around Bastogne, and the battle raged there for a week. Montgomery did not keep still. He evacuated St. Vith and withdrew the American Seventh Corps into reserve. On January 3, he mounted a counteroffensive against the Germans.

By that time Kluge's troops were pretty well through. On January 8, the Germans pulled back and the Battle of the Bulge was over.

Comment

Even though the fierce counterattack of Hitler's army failed in its final objective to reach Antwerp, it did indeed rupture the Allied lines by striking a telling blow at the seam of the front lines where British and American command structures linked up. In addition to Hitler's success in temporarily separating the two huge commands, he also exploited the psychological differences between the various individual commanders. The Allied commanders' somewhat conflicting moves canceled out a quick and forceful response that might have saved many lives.

Although Montgomery recovered first and moved with precision and intelligence, his failure to communicate his actions to Eisenhower left the supreme commander in the dark as to his colleague's intentions. The result was time-consuming, confusing and ineffective.

In military operations, there is a vastly reduced chance for success without a unified command—that is, one person.

HORIZONTAL STRUCTURE EXAMINED

The question naturally arises: Is there such a thing as horizontal structure for authority? Actually there could be, and in some instances there is. In the situation we have just reviewed, the supreme commander, Eisenhower, was the apex of the command. Under him were a handful of officers, with the authority going down from Eisenhower to the others. Inasmuch as each of the generals directly under Eisenhower had large numbers of troops, the authority in some instances traveled in an almost horizontal direction rather than a vertical one because of the division of command.

The problem is that in a horizontal structure, authority is fragmented and tends not to be pure and clear. When authority is clouded it becomes less than effective. By its very nature, a military unit must exert sharp and decisive authority. When an order comes from the top, it travels down cleanly without change from command level to command level. Such an order must be obeyed for the operation to be successful.

The only logical manner in which an army can function is in a structure that allows vertical movement of authority.

Let's move from warfare of a military kind to warfare of a corporate kind. In corporate combat, the same truth seems evident—there must be unity of command flowing from the top down through all the personnel working in the company.

The buck, as Harry Truman was fond of reminding reporters, stops here.

THE FRAGMENTATION OF THE LINE OF COMMAND

Despite the seeming obviousness of the principle of unity of command, there have been various attempts to fragment it and restructure the corporate entity in a different way. One of these particular methods is called matrix management.

Was there a reason for experimentation with the traditional command structure?

Actually there *was* a need for a new approach because of the increasingly complex realities of American business in the postwar era:

- The increase in conglomerates, with the assimilation of dozens of different types of business entities, service and manufacturing concerns under one head, made it almost impossible to function without some kind of dual responsibility.
- Interdependent product lines proliferating in certain successful companies also created problems that could be solved only by blurring responsibility and authority.

These types of changes created problems for management. Just as military authority is vertical, so is the conventional, classic form of organizational structure. In the long chain of command—through research and development, through manufacturing, through marketing and so on—each has a centralized control.

However, another type of command is possible without centralized control. This is a horizontal configuration with separate responsibilities for products and markets. And this is the type that has sometimes proven successful with certain companies which have large numbers of products and services to offer.

The functional type—vertical—avoids duplication, with one research and development division, one manufacturing division and one marketing division, and provides for as efficient use as possible of all corporate resources. Inside such a structure, each function can make full use of specialization, thus improving efficiency.

The functional organization finds it difficult, however, to handle a large number of diverse products, targeted at different kinds of customers with wide-ranging needs and demands. It cannot usually perform as well as if it produces one product that it sells to one kind of customer.

One solution is to construct an organization with a product-market orientation and set it up in a different configuration. With each product having its own research and development division, its own manufacturing division and its own marketing division, the company can provide service for a variety of its customers on a more individualized basis, even though it is not really as efficient as a company with centralized control.

The classic matrix management structure resembles a large rectangle that looks like a graph. The horizontal layers are product 1, product

2, product 3 and so on, with each layer divided by vertical lines of function running through each business labeled Manufacturing Manager, Marketing Manager, Financial Manager, Administrative Manager and so on.

At the top of the compartment sits the chief executive officer, with a line extending down to all these separate functions and businesses. What is obvious to anyone used to the classic vertical structure of management is that there is no single point of responsibility or authority.

For example, in a typical vertical structure, there is only one research and development section, or whatever. In matrix management, there are research and development sections for each separate product. There is a very good reason for this; in today's world, one company may manufacture an extensive product line with items in no way related to one another; each product must have its own separate functional system to make and sell it.

But this of course creates a problem in responsibility and authority. The CEO cannot control directly down through each function. The lieutenant in charge of each product can essentially override, contradict or ignore him. It is a two-boss (or more) dual-responsibility system, but no product manager has authority to order the manufacturing manager to do something differently.

Let's take a look at a case history of this new type of conglomerate management and see what kind of command problems exist under such a system. Indeed, unity of command here is more recognizable in the breach than in the observance.

CORPORATE CASE HISTORY

TEXAS INSTRUMENTS (1982–83)

The Objective

In April 1982, J. Fred Bucy, president of Texas Instruments, one of the fastest growing and most profitable electronics product companies in the country, made a startling announcement to his stockholders at the annual meeting.

"Matrix management has been sunk," he told them as they sat there in shock.

The matrix approach fragmented both people and resources and diffused authority to the point where managers could not carry out their program responsibilities effectively.

The trouble, he went on, lay in the fact that with the success of the company, and with the increase in size and complexity of TI's matrix system, there had been an accompanying separation of authority from the resources to do the job. In other words, the system, which had been set up to develop a workable modus operandi, had failed to support its objectives, effective program teams. Program execution was suffering. What had been workable once to fulfill corporate objectives was now unworkable. A new system would have to be substituted.

As the company had grown, there had been trouble on the operating side. Large centralized support organizations had grown up with increased resources. But the managers supposed to handle the resources had not been able to do so.

"The manager was a negotiator between support organizations," Bucy said, and was not in *control* at all.

The strategy would be to scrap the matrix system and return more or less to the type of strategies and philosophies of management that had made the company one of the giants of the industry in a very short time.

R. Michael Lockerd, vice president in charge of strategic planning at TI, had this to say about the problem:

> One of our errors was we had the tendency to substitute mechanics for thought. People would fill out forms thinking they were doing strategies. It was strategy by cookbook.

The Tactics

The balance of Bucy's message promised that there would be big changes at TI, a reorganization of company management, the breaking of the matrix, the creation of a new organizational concept at the corporate, product and development levels.

All product managers would now have authority for their product lines, as if each were a separate company. Under the matrix structure, product managers were forced to deal with managers within the matrix, as negotiators, to schedule production, assembly, research and marketing support for their products. Now they would have full charge.

Comment

Matrix management almost sank TI. A professor of management and organization at the University of Southern California calls it "the kiss of death" for an unprepared company to rush into matrix management. Management consultant John Humphrey, chairman of the Forum Corporation in Boston, Massachusetts, views matrix management this way:

> Matrix management is good in that it recognizes that two or more lines of authority in a company must exercise control over the same resources and negotiate for their use. It also enables a company to focus strongly on more than one direction at a time, to process a great deal of information and respond to changing situations more quickly.
>
> But matrix structures also create problems since they create multiple chains of command, different and often conflicting priorities for individuals, and different demands. Even if a clear definition of roles and procedures has been established, it is of little use unless people follow them. Because a manager has no direct control over the people involved in a task, he cannot rely on directive to ensure that the plan will be carried out.
>
> It has been our experience that organizations too often try to slide into a matrix. Companies reason that people will need to feel out their new roles and that their roles and priorities will gradually be worked out. What generally happens, however, is that people working in this new ambiguous structure become so frustrated and angry that the new organization is severely handicapped, if not totally obliterated before its purpose can be clarified.

Comment

The problem at Texas Instruments, and at some other companies that have taken up matrix management, is that the system directly violates the concept of unity of command. In other words, with the various heads arguing among themselves, or arguing with the chief executive officer, there is no final decision possible in a way that could ensure prompt results.

The adding of the horizontal lines to the vertical lines of authority already involved in a company is frightening. That means that the chief of any division might retain the responsibility for the merchandising of his particular product or service, but have no authority over the marketing division needed to ensure the effective operation of that department!

DUAL-RESPONSIBILITY MANAGEMENT ELSEWHERE

General Electric was an early advocate of matrix management, although at the time it was tried it was called simply "dual-responsibility management." During the years of World War II, GE grew vertically along classic lines of function—autonomous divisions of sales, engineering, manufacturing and accounting. The problem was that GE's product line expanded and widened considerably. Not only was the company making light bulbs and toasters, but radios, television sets and even enormous industrial turbines. What the company did was to select a group of product managers; these managers went out to the various functional managers and there tried to procure the resources their products needed.

In other words, there were go-betweens that acted as liaisons between divisions and functions.

This was fundamentally a role of weak overlay, but soon the product manager at GE became a dominant figure after the company decided to concentrate on "strategic business."

A WORLD-CONGLOMERATE EXAMPLE

At International Telephone and Telegraph, it worked in another way. ITT was a worldwide conglomerate, but it was organized in a slightly different fashion from the normal vertical structure.

The CEO held all division managers accountable for day-to-day profitability—no matter what they were responsible for manufacturing and selling. On the other hand, he held the corporate staff's worldwide product planners accountable and insisted they continue to increase sales growth.

When accountability overlapped or conflicted, the CEO called both managers on the carpet to make a final decision—but only in case of conflict that threatened to reduce productivity and profits.

Nevertheless, in May 1983 the company was reorganized in an effort to consolidate the research and marketing efforts of ITT's highly independent subsidiaries. Each of four independent "companies" was reorganized with a specific head for each.

"ITT's strength has always been its participation in so many national markets," one former executive of the company said. "But its strength was also the cause of its problems, especially fragmentation of research and development."

By adjusting the organizational structure, ITT sought to realize its management strength among its subsidiaries. A basically horizontal setup was being strengthened in a vertical manner.

In short, its chain of command, in the military sense, was being reimposed with a clarification of specific responsibilities—and a precise definition of who had what authority. The fact that ITT's CEO graduated from West Point may have prompted him to take this action as soon as he did.

nine

SIMPLICITY

If you can't explain it, you don't understand it.

—Chuck Knight

One of the most influential philosophers of the Middle Ages was born in the tiny village of Ockham in Surrey, England. He took the name William of Occam (Latinized from Ockham) and became a theological philosopher at Oxford University.

Occam avoided complicated generalities and espoused simplicities. He cut through the gobbledygook of theological pontification with the keen edge of reason. His principle—that of economy of thought—is called "Occam's Razor," the razor used to slash through the verbiage of religious dogma.

His theory: "A plurality (of reasons) should not be posited without necessity." In other words, all speculation about religion should be based on simplicity. It was the lack of simplicity that for years had trapped thinkers of all kinds and discouraged free thought.

Simplicity of thought works in military situations as well as in business situations—the best possible way to avoid misunderstanding and confusion. It is essential, for example, that all military plans and orders to subordinates be as simple as possible to be understood and carried out successfully. That, in a nutshell, is the military principle of simplicity. In order to keep things simple, the Marine Corps teaches its officers and noncoms the five-paragraph order. All inclusive, it is simplicity itself:

- Situation: Where we are, where the enemy is
- Mission: What our objective is
- Execution: How we are going to maneuver
- Administration: How we will resupply beans, bandaids and bullets
- Command and Control: What signals will be used.

SIMPLICITY IN TACTICS AND MANEUVERS

Simplicity does not mean that the best military expedient is to march in a straight line to get from one point to another in the quickest time. The strategy and tactics may not be quite so simple.

As we have seen, it is sometimes better to attack in an indirect manner rather than in a direct manner. An envelopment maneuver, which covers a great deal more ground, is often superior to a direct frontal attack.

It is the execution of the maneuver that must be simple. Subordinate commanders must understand the plan to carry it out.

For example, an attack may be quite complicated in planning. A group may be required to make a complicated, circuitous route to arrive at a point from which to launch an attack on an enemy force. Yet if the leader of the group understands the route and can give clear, concise orders to those in his command, then the execution of the maneuver is essentially one of *simplicity*.

Let's take a look at a recent military action that was a model of simplicity in execution, and because of its essential simplicity was destined for success almost from the moment of its conception.

MILITARY CASE HISTORY

LIBERATION OF THE FALKLAND ISLANDS (MAY–JUNE 1982)

The Objective

For years, Argentina and Great Britain had been arguing about the possession of the Falkland Islands some 250 miles from the southeastern tip of Argentina. The 2000 people who herded sheep and lived on the islands preferred to remain under British control.

But on April 2, 1982, between 4000 and 5000 Argentinian troops stormed the islands and overwhelmed the 84 British Royal marines who guarded them.

Also seized were South Georgia and South Sandwich Islands, some 200 miles southeast of the Falklands.

There were no British forces nearby. The government surrendered to the Argentine commander and the islanders were kept under arms. Although the Falklands lay 8000 miles to the south of Great Britain, Prime Minister Margaret Thatcher promptly assembled a naval task force of some 8000 troops and set sail for the islands—a voyage that would take approximately two weeks. The task force consisted of two aircraft carriers, destroyers, frigates, landing ships, commandos and a number of regular troops.

The *Queen Elizabeth II*, one of the world's largest tourist steamships, was commandeered by the British government to carry troops to the Falklands.

The objective of the task force was to seize the islands from the Argentinians and return them to English control.

The Strategy

There was little secrecy about the coming invasion attempt. The best way to proceed, the British commander decided, was to mount an extremely simple and classic amphibious invasion of the islands.

The first move was to prepare the area for attack. To do this, the British imposed a naval blockade on the area. The government treatened to sink any Argentine ship that came within 200 miles fo the Falkland Islands after April 11. Being cut off from outside help and resupply had an immediate and predictable impact on the morale of the Argentine soldiers. They began a long period of living on dwindling supplies of food and ammunition.

The second move was to gain a foothold somewhere in the target area—but not to attack the entrenched Argentinians at Port Stanley, the most populous city. Instead, the British targeted and took South Georgia Island. The invasion was a simple maneuver. Advance troops were landed from helicopters flown from the British task force still steaming down from England. An Argentinian submarine was sunk in the encounter.

The third preliminary move was to soften up the primary objective—Port Stanley—by bombardment from the sea and from the air. On May 1, a predawn raid pounded the city, and other raids were made on Goose Green, a smaller settlement some 25 miles east of Port Stanley.

With the possibility of counterattack by the Argentinians from the direction of South Georgia curtailed by the British invasion in the first days of combat, the primary objective was now isolated to the main Falkland Islands. There were two of them, West Falkland and East Falkland, with small islands surrounding them. Port Stanley lies on the eastern portion of East Falkland. West Falkland is thinly populated. Between the two large islands stretches Falkland Sound, a strait only a few miles wide.

The strategy decided on was classic in its simplicity: to approach the objective indirectly in strength, rather than attack head on and risk heavy losses in a landing at Port Stanley. A secondary tactic was necessary: to secure Falkland Sound so that once in place on East Falkland, the British invasion forces would not be surprised at their rear by the Argentinians coming from the sound.

With the strait between the islands secured, the British could then land at Port San Carlos, Goose Green and Darwin on West Falkland. They would then join forces to sweep across the island toward Port Stanley on the east coast.

The Tactics

This called for more softening-up tactics. On May 9, the British warships bombarded Port Stanley with 4.5-inch guns. This shelling continued. On May 11, the British cleared Falkland Sound. Air and sea battles continued. Bombs were dropped by the British to curtail use of the airstrips for defense.

After the preliminary softening up, the British began a series of hit-and-run raids on Pebble Island, a small prominence off West Falkland. The probe was intended to test out Argentinian resistance. There seemed to be none.

Now the way was paved for the first move of the invasion of the Falkland Islands.

On May 21, the British landed at Port San Carlos, on the northern tip of East Falkland, and established a beachhead there. Four days later the San Carlos beachhead had been enlarged to a zone of 60 square miles. Inside that zone the British massed 5000 paratroopers and ground troops.

Bombing of Port Stanley continued.

Now the stage was set for the final attack on Port Stanley. The distance from Port San Carlos to Port Stanley was more than 50 miles of extremely difficult terrain. The Argentinians knew the British would not attack them over those rugged hills. But, indeed, the opposite was true too. The Argentinians holding Port Stanley could not move across to attack the British at Port San Carlos.

The strategy was, of course, to move the British troops down to Darwin and Goose Green and then make a wide curve to the east toward Port Stanley. And to prepare the way for the troops at Port San Carlos, the British planned hits on Goose Green and Darwin.

On May 27, British paratroopers took Darwin and Goose

Green. Both settlements had been bolstered by Argentinian reserves when the Argentinians had deduced what the British were up to. The reserve troops numbered about 1400 in the two settlements.

British paratroopers, about 600 strong for each target, were dropped onto Darwin and Goose Green. After a short and furious fight, the 1400 exhausted and hungry Argentinians surrendered.

Almost immediately, the British troops waiting at Port San Carlos received their marching orders. They streamed down the western side of East Falkland toward the two captured settlements.

Meanwhile, British naval guns bombarded Port Stanley. At the same time, with the Argentinians pinned down trying to fight off the British bombardment, the *Queen Elizabeth II* arrived at Port San Carlos with a large contingent of fresh troops, offloading them immediately. These troops joined the march to Darwin and Goose Green.

The British ground forces were moving swiftly now. On June 1, they had secured an extremely strategic position on Mount Kent, only 10 miles from Port Stanley. On June 7, the British were only 5 miles from their final objective.

By June 8, an estimated 9000 British soldiers were on the island. There were, according to British intelligence, about 6000 to 7000 Argentinians isolated at Port Stanley.

On June 11, the British were fighting pockets of resistance on the outskirts of Port Stanley. The naval guns continued to clobber the port city. Then, on June 14, the Argentinian commander in charge finally surrendered in the face of enormous potential losses.

It was all over.

Comment

The assault on the Falkland Islands was a case of classic simplicity. Both sides—and the world—knew pretty much what was going to happen. But the British eventually achieved a concentration of mass at the right time and the right place—enough to overwhelm the Argentinians defending Port Stanley. The blockade around the Falklands paid off. The Argentines could not send in more troops to help resist the British advance on Port Stanley.

The innate simplicity of the invasion campaign was amazingly decisive. But there was a great deal more to the success of the Falkland liberation than clarity of orders. The British were trained and knew what they were doing. The Argentines were emotionally ready, but they had never fought a major battle and were completely untested in combat.

Military historian James F. Dunningan wrote:

> Good infantry is worth three or more times as much as inferior infantry. Courage and fanaticism are not enough. British troops attacked larger Argentine forces and won because they had the initiative, planned carefully, trained hard, and were well led. Superior morale and reputation, moreover, can be decisive weapons. The British have a long reputation for winning. The Argentines have not fought a war in this century. All things being equal, the side with the superior reputation will inevitably win.

In this case, they did. They knew they were superior in training to the Argentines. That was the reason the British commander in charge of the invasion could draw up such a simple and bold strategy—a step-by-step chalkboard game plan to drive the Argentinians off the Falkland Islands. But there was another reason for the British success: Their soldiers were all volunteers; the Argentinians were mostly conscripts.

SMALL IS SOMETIMES BETTER

Simplicity—the lesson of Occam's Razor—is a must not only in military combat, but in corporate combat as well, where it is sometimes referred to as the KISS principle (Keep It Simple, Stupid). The concept of corporate simplicity has always been the handwriting on the wall— if anyone bothered to read it. The extinct dinosaur syndrome was not confined to history, or to the animal kingdom. It operated as well in the halls of commerce.

Yet during the 1960s and 1970s, when the move to acquire companies and expand started, many corporate commanders deliberately ignored lessons from the past and began to merge and acquire and enlarge their companies into enormous conglomerates, with little or no synergism between business units.

THE CASE OF BEATRICE FOODS

For a good 10 years in the 1970s, Beatrice Foods had a growing spree that was unprecedented in its own history. It acquired company after company until finally the Chicago firm was a $10-billion-a-year conglomerate.

Beatrice's products included a number of diverse items—from orange juice to select luggage. The number of companies within the conglomerate was fewer than 100, but possibly nearing the point of unmanageability.

Beatrice, like a lot of other enormous conglomerates under the stress of high interest rates and a slumping economy, began to sell off some of its divisions in 1982. The idea was to dump the unprofitable firms in order to reverse the trend and to reverse money-flow problems.

THE BUSINESS OF DIVESTITURE

Divestiture tended to be a dirty word in the industry. Whether true or not, it was interpreted to mean that the company involved in divesting itself of one of its divisions or one of its companies had made a mistake either in acquiring the company in the first place or in running the company under its umbrella of control.

But in 1982, corporate divestitures became the thing to do. The watchwords were "back to basics," and unprofitable entities were shut down, spun off or liquidated.

Beatrice, like many of its competitors, planned to unload some 50 of its numerous divisions by the end of 1983. But Beatrice was only one of a long list of other huge conglomerates that had made up their minds to divest. For example:

- American Can, originally a company that manufactured tin cans and packages and containers, became a large conglomerate involving the manufacture of all kinds of paper and cardboard products. Recently it began to sell off its paper products business to concentrate not on tin cans, or on containers at all, but on the more profitable financial services business.
- Black & Decker Manufacturing had bought McCulloch chain saw company, but when it began to lose money in the 1970s recession, the parent suffered its first loss since 1933. It sold off the chain saw company.
- Charter Company was originally an oil and refining business, but had acquired a number of companies dealing in other services and products. One of its least profitable divisions was an insurance subsidiary. It recently decided to divest itself of that division.
- Du Pont, the chemical and chemical products conglomerate, recently sold off the oil and gas fields belonging to its Conoco division in order to retrench and move back into its original interest—chemicals—and to comply with certain legal requirements imposed by the government.
- Esmark, one of the most active of the conglomerates, recently sold off its energy holdings and its meat-packing division.
- Firestone Tire & Rubber Company, which manufactured the products in its name for years, had acquired numbers of companies making passenger restraint systems, phone products and steel products of all kinds. Recently it began to divest itself of companies that did not fit in with its original concept: tires and related rubber-goods activities.
- Gulf & Western Industries had gone through a huge acquisition phase when it became one of the big conglomerates noted for its movie business that also included companies manufacturing cigars and selling paper, insurance, cement, zinc, real estate, building materials and other products. It recently sold off its insurance and real estate companies, cigar and paper companies to concentrate on its more prosperous sectors.
- Quaker Oats, which started out as a breakfast food company, but which became interested in such esoteric ventures as toys, chemicals and even video games, began to get rid of its companies that had nothing to do with food. It soon began to guide itself into a conglomerate involving brand-name consumer products only.

GOING AGAINST THE PRINCIPLE OF SIMPLICITY

Those are only a few of a long list of conglomerates being "deconglomeratized." The divestiture bug has bitten a large number of companies—and with a vengeance. It had to be so, because the bigness of a conglomerate did not necessarily pay off in profits that were proportionately big.

What the business community did was to fly in the face of the old military principle of simplicity.

The trend toward simplicity in industry really started several years ago when, as mentioned before, the interest rates were so high it was difficult or impossible for companies to borrow to bail themselves out of the recession. It was often cheaper for a conglomerate to get rid of a division that was not hauling its own weight than to borrow money to aid the venture.

In a *Forbes* story on divestitures, Fred R. Bleakely wrote:

At the same time, corporate philosophy increasingly emphasized efficiency and simplicity. Managements wanted to concentrate on what they know how to do best.

Bleakely's use of the word "simplicity" pretty well sums it up.

ten

SECURITY

All warfare is based on deception. Hence, when able to attack, we must seem unable; when using our forces, we must seem inactive; when we are near, we must make the enemy believe that we are away; when far away, we must make him believe we are near. Hold out baits to entice the enemy. Feign disorder, and crush him.

—SUN TZU

Four men climbed out of a rent-a-limo in Oakhurst, California, and walked in formation up to the front entrance of Sierra On-Line company's facilities. They were dressed in civilian uniform, each wearing a dark, conservatively cut, three-piece suit. Explaining that they were from International Business Machines headquarters, they asked to see the person in charge of Sierra On-Line.

When the president ushered them into his office, one of the group explained that the four were just passing through the area and had decided to drop in to see the plant, which had signed a contract to develop software for IBM.

That brought a smile of amusement from the company's president, who could tell at a glance that four men in three-piece suits were certainly not present in the area to take part in recreational activities at nearby Yosemite National Park as their statement implied. Nevertheless, he made them welcome and took them through the plant for what they assured him would be only a casual visit.

Casual?

Within minutes the men from Big Blue were banging away at the locks on the doors to special rooms, carefully sifting through the refuse in wastebaskets to test the shredding devices and even rattling the security bars on filing cabinets in the offices.

What these four men found apparently satisfied them, and their report back to headquarters approved Sierra On-Line's security measures to preserve the industrial electronics secrets that IBM was so intent on keeping. Nevertheless, within a short time, the men from Big Blue were back again, going through the same kind of checkout on security precautions, doing the entire drill once again.

DISINFORMATION—ONE KEY TO SECURITY

Outsiders—that is, those who have never had the privilege of working for Big Blue on a contractual basis—claim that the company is and always has been paranoid about security. For example, when IBM contracts to have a piece of a certain unit manufactured by a supplier, it only imparts enough information to the company to allow it to fabricate the piece itself. The supplying company has no idea what the finished product is going to look like if the product has not yet been introduced to the public.

In fact, it has been claimed that in some instances IBM has purposely leaked fake rumors about a product to be introduced in the future, discrete details that help build up an extrapolated picture of a nonproduct quite unlike what IBM is *really* going to make.

"I'm convinced they have a disinformation division," one supplier was quoted as saying. "You simply don't talk when you are an IBM supplier," another executive said. "It's not good for your health."

COMPARTMENTALIZE FOR SECURITY

Because competition has been so intense in the personal computer business, IBM's security system got its severest test during the early 1980s. Its main competitor, Apple, had already introduced the personal computer and was going great guns in selling its product to the awakened public. So were other entrants into the newly formed personal computer market.

IBM did not manufacture the components of its planned personal computer. Parts were made *outside* the company. However, the assembly was performed at the IBM plant in Boca Raton. None of the competition had any idea what the finished product would look like until the first unit rolled off the assembly line in Florida—and yet literally hundreds of companies throughout the country were manufacturing parts of the complex electronic computer.

The introduction of the IBM PC was an example of total security on the part of Big Blue in an industry that is rife with stolen secrets and plundered product parts.

• • •

Security in business has always been an important issue in the successful performance of a corporation. In fact, most corporate security plans are based on military security systems. Early in the history of warfare, the military realized it could not survive in any battle if the enemy had an awareness, or even the slightest inkling, of what was in the minds of the commander in regard to disposition of troops, supplies or other impedimenta.

In military parlance, security demands complete adherence at all levels of command. The slogan during World War II, "Loose lips sink ships," is a good example of the thoroughness to which the military must go to protect its vital secrets and of the seriousness of secrecy during times of war. Security is essential to the preservation of combat power.

During battle, security must be continuously maintained to prevent surprise by the enemy, to preserve freedom of action and to prevent the enemy from obtaining any information about friendly forces.

SECURITY AND INTELLIGENCE

Security is actually the opposite side of the coin of one of the military's most important activities—the gathering of intelligence about the enemy. Security *prevents* the enemy from gathering information that might be detrimental to the successful prosecution of a coming or ongoing battle.

Security might be considered a negative quality, and intelligence a positive quality. Both security and intelligence are essential to the successful end of any battle. In most commands the gathering of intelligence and the prevention of enemy assaults on security are separate branches of the same division: intelligence. In Britain, these departments are called MI5 and MI6, showing the close affinity of these disparate sections.

One of the most memorable lapses of security occurred on December 7, 1941, when the Japanese flew all the way over the Pacific Ocean and bombed the American military installations at Pearl Harbor, bringing about the United States entry into World War II.

Although American intelligence did have information that the enemy was going to strike, the cumbersome machinery of the military juggernaut was not able to move on that information in time to prevent the debacle.

There is still controversy over the actual details of this fatal flaw in security, and perhaps the final disposition of blame will never be made.

On the positive side, the Normandy landings in June 1944 were successfully engineered because of abnormally complicated stratagems to confuse and bewilder the Germans about the exact location of the main thrust of the invasion assault. Disinformation was deliberately fed to the Germans through underground enemy agents, fake code messages it was known the Germans could break and force-fed gossip by German friendlies in France.

In fact, an actor who resembled General Bernard Montgomery was even sent to North Africa to draw Nazi attention to the Mediterranean as a possible landing site. A feint actually occurred there on the French Riviera simultaneously with the Normandy invasion. A false American army group was set up on England's southeastern coast with dummy tanks to fool German air reconnaissance. Bombing raids were made on Calais, France, Holland and even Norway to make the Germans believe that each of those targets might be the primary objective.

Although Hitler had uncannily guessed right, and the landings were made at Normandy, he dithered and delayed action, feeling that the Normandy beachhead might be a probe with the real force hitting Calais. In the end, the invasion achieved complete surprise, and in that first day, 155,000 troops were ashore, bloodied but established within a beachhead of 80 square miles at Normandy.

THE WORKING OF GOOD SECURITY

These two examples of military security bring up several questions:

- How does military security work?
- Who is responsible for it?
- How can security be adjusted to fool the enemy?
- How does one commander breach the security of another commander to find out vital secrets and take advantage of the enemy's weaknesses?

The study and understanding of security depends on the study and understanding of intelligence—the opposite of security. Having seen how both faulty and ideal security can operate in vital military situations, the obvious approach now is to look at the basic strategy and tactics of intelligence and disinformation, with a classic example of the gathering of military intelligence during World War I.

INTELLIGENCE AND THE MILITARY

From the earliest days of civilization, combat of any kind has depended on the proper gathering and assessment of intelligence about the enemy's strength and weakness. In the case of one individual in combat with another, such an intelligence evaluation can be made visually, including a quick assessment of the capability of the opponent—how muscular he is, what kind of weapons he possesses, what kind of backup he has and so on.

Intelligence assessment is an important part of any military engagement, as has been shown. All scouting missions, preliminary engagements, reports from the lines and briefings and debriefings come under the overall umbrella of intelligence gathering.

Intelligence deals with all the things that should be known before any course of action is initiated—in military undertakings, in business endeavors, in personal decisions.

Security, the opposite of intelligence, tries to deal with the same things from the standpoint of thwarting the enemy's intelligence-gathering operations. When the enemy's intelligence is superior, the commander's security is inferior; when the enemy's security is superior, the commander's intelligence gathering is inferior.

There are actually two different kinds of intelligence agents. One gathers information and conveys it to his masters. The other prevents the leaking of information to the enemy. The first type of agent belongs to intelligence; the second to security. Both distinctions are arbitrary. Many agents work in both intelligence and security according to assignment.

SPIES COME IN FIVE FLAVORS

According to Allen Dulles, former director of the Central Intelligence Agency, there are five different kinds of agents:

- the inside agent
- the native agent
- the double agent
- the expendable agent
- the penetration agent

An inside agent is an agent actually a resident, although not necessarily a native, of the country from which the intelligence information is to be obtained by the intelligence-gathering country.

A native agent is also called an agent in place. The native agent, as the name implies, is usually a citizen of the country where the intelligence is being gathered. The difference between an inside agent and a native agent is the country of origin of each.

A double agent is an agent who works for both sides, taking money from the information-gathering country for pieces of information delivered and taking money from the country in which he is operating to funnel out only information desired by the country being spied on.

An expendable agent is an agent used by an information-gathering country to feed disinformation to the enemy; when such an agent is captured, the enemy obtains disinformation before doing away with him, because, by his very job category, he is expendable.

The penetration agent, also called a living agent, is a mobile agent who goes into the enemy country, extracts information on the move there and then comes out to return to his own country, carrying the information intact rather than risking interception in exchange.

The only reason these types of agents are discussed in detail is that all of them can be used with varying degrees of success in business as well as in military combat. Let's take a look at a few stories of intelligence-gathering in military situations to get some idea of the invaluable assistance espionage can afford to a fighting country.

The Saga of Charles Lucieto

In World War I, the Germans had been experimenting with poison gas, trying to come up with a weapon that could win the war for them in a kind of instant gambit. The Germans had always been obsessed with a "secret weapon" that could make them masters of the world.

Fritz Haber, a clever scientist, perfected a system for synthesizing ammonia from nitrogen and hydrogen. His process became the basis of a most successful commercial fertilizer. When the Germans realized that they needed a secret weapon for the coming war, the German war staff came to him for help.

Borrowing an idea from H. G. Wells's *War of the Worlds,* published in 1898, Haber came up with chlorine gas. Within six months, he had perfected a mask to protect the German troops who would be dispensing the gas and was ready to make use of his secret weapon.

However, his moves were under observation by an intelligence agent of the French government. Charles Lucieto was posing as a mechanic in Germany and, following various rumors, he located the factory where the chlorine gas was being made in Mannheim. There he found huge containers in which it was to be shipped to the Krupp arms works.

In Essen, Lucieto befriended a policeman of the Krupp security force. His new friend explained that Krupp was getting chlorine gas and packaging it into artillery shells. An argument ensued, Lucieto professing disbelief. The security man made a friendly bet and sneaked Lucieto in to show him an experimental gas shoot.

As Lucieto watched, a naval battery fired gas-loaded shells at a herd of sheep on a hillside. A huge green cloud settled on the animals, and they fell dead almost immediately. The grass around them withered.

Lucieto paid off the bet and professed enthusiasm for the secret weapon. "Do you think I could get a tiny shell fragment to keep as a souvenir?" The Krupp man got it for him.

Within three days, the shell fragment was in the hands of a Parisian chemist, with the chemicals on it under analysis.

By the time Haber's weapon was used on April 22, 1915, at Ypres, the French and British were working on their own version. Gas warfare was under way in earnest.

•   •   •

Along with information-gathering, force-feeding disinformation is the next most important type of military espionage. The activity that surrounded the Normandy invasion in June 1944 has already been mentioned. But the really classic use of disinformation occurred a year earlier during the North African campaign in 1943.

The Saga of "Major Martin"

The Allies had taken North Africa after an intense struggle against the Germans and were preparing their next move. The plan was to cross over through Sicily to Italy and northward into Germany. But in spite of the obviousness of the strategy, the Allies wanted to confuse the enemy, to make the Germans think the attack would be somewhere other than Sicily.

British intelligence came up with a plan that might have been nurtured in a spy thriller by Ian Fleming. They obtained the corpse of a recently deceased civilian and dressed it up in the uniform of a British major. In the pockets of the uniform they put fake ID papers, calling cards and odds and ends that authenticated the corpse as that of a certain "Major Martin."

Agents also chained and locked a briefcase to the wrist of the corpse. In the briefcase were planted papers purported to be correspondence to General Harold Alexander in Tunisia from the Imperial General Staff in London. The papers hinted at an Allied plan to invade Southern Europe through Sardinia and Greece—a two-pronged attack that entirely contradicted the obvious Allied plan up through Sicily and Italy.

Intelligence then floated the body out of a British submarine near the southwest coast of Spain in the proximity of the town of Huelva between the Portuguese border and Gibraltar. The submarine lingered long enough to make sure the body washed up on shore at a "proper" place—and it did, right on time and target.

Almost immediately the papers on the corpse found their way to the proper German intelligence agents and the documents were then carefully shipped on to Berlin. There German intelligence authenticated them and apparently believed the facts in the papers.

Proof of their acceptance of the fake accident that had happened to "Major Martin" occurred some weeks later when Hitler allocated one armored division to Greece and instructed Italian dictator Benito Mussolini to reinforce the Italian garrison on Sardinia.

USING INTELLIGENCE IN CORPORATE COMBAT

Intelligence can be used by business as well as by the military to prepare a more successful type of marketing operation. In fact, most corporations use both intelligence and disinformation tactics every day in their own research and development and marketing.

Many large companies make no secret of asking employees to collect intelligence at all levels regarding competitiors and competitive products. They include:

- Celanese
- Del Monte
- Emerson Electric
- Ford Motor Company
- General Electric
- Gillette
- J. C. Penney
- Kraft
- Rockwell International
- Union Carbide

Of course there are many others; almost any company does a little judicious snooping now and then. There are companies actually engaged in *teaching* corporation executives to winnow out information from the competition. One of them is Washington Resources Limited, which recently ran a seminar on spying.

Operation Crush

Quite recently Intel Corporation, manufacturer of electronics products, learned that Motorola Corporation was developing a microprocessor chip. Intel sent its company engineers out to their own customers to try to find out what Motorola was up to. These customers were the ones who might be potential buyers of Motorola's new chip.

From debriefing reports of their engineers, Intel put together an accurate picture of the competing chip's design details. It then instituted Operation Crush, a sales campaign to get customers to specify that they used Intel's chip in their products. In this way Intel managed to forestall the impact of Motorola's new chip on their own business. Their sales campaign proved so effective that they managed to acquire Xerox and IBM as customers!

Operation Schmeir

Cordis Corporation of Miami came up with a very good model pacemaker in 1980, one that was competitively better than most of the competition. Nevertheless, Cordis discovered that its sales were lagging behind those of the competition, and even sinking—particularly among elderly retired wearers.

Discreet inquiries by company experts soon uncovered the fact that the competition was using every possible facet of salesmanship to get cardiologists to recommend their products. In some instances there were exchanges of expensive cars, boats and other luxury items. Cordis did not fight back in kind, but simply inaugurated a hard-sell program of image-making to fight the guerrilla tactics of the competition.

•   •   •

Both these companies actually learned what their sales problems were by means of intelligence-gathering tactics. It is obvious that intelligence-gathering works on several different levels in the corporate world.

The most apparent level is the one that has just been explored—intelligence gleaned to determine current sales patterns in marketing and what, if anything, is causing the competition to surge ahead. No company really wants another to know how much money it is making. A corporation therefore tries to keep these figures secret—as secret as possible.

In the case of newspaper circulation or movie theater ticket sales, these figures become newsworthy items immediately and are sent out to the media for publication to tout the success of a production and to encourage future ticket sales. Nevertheless, other cost factors are kept very much in the dark.

MARKETING RESEARCH AND ANALYSIS

Marketing ventures depend on advance intelligence in order to make proper estimates about the potential of a certain product in a particular area, geographical or generic. This type of predicting, much like the early prophecies of the ancients who asked the gods for advice, is based on certain hard facts and clever extrapolations of these facts into statistical charts.

One of the most important concepts of intelligence on this level is the capability of the company itself and its prospective product, and of the competition. Not only are a company's own figures checked and rechecked, but the opposition's figures are sought out or pieced together by deductions involving knowns and intuited unknowns.

The "secrets" of industrial processes are always a prime target on intelligence operations hired by the competition. Today such secrets are of course protected by patents and laws of infringement. Nevertheless, the stealing and selling of industrial secrets has become a big business among thieves and spies.

Fashion designs are a typical target for immediate fencing for profit. So are automobile designs and new engineering breakthroughs and many other innovations, substitutions and new ways of doing things.

The Secret in the Flowered Hat

Industrial spying is nothing new. In 2640 B.C., the Chinese began using silk to weave fabulously comfortable and expensive garments. No one outside China knew that silk thread was not grown but actually spun by a worm. If anyone had known, no one would have believed it anyway.

The story goes that the secret remained in China for years until a princess fell in love with a man who lived in India—a traveling merchant who spent much of his time buying and selling in China.

The princess's parents were against this affair with a common salesman, of course, and forbade the marriage. The princess loved the merchant, but he was not about to risk his life to smuggle her over the lines to India. However, when she agreed to give him the secret of silkmaking, he decided to risk it and arranged for her safe trip to India.

The princess arrived at her lover's home dressed in a wonderful flowered hat. In the flowers on the hat she had hidden some of the silkworms. She showed the hat and the worms to her lover. What was at first disbelief finally turned to belief. The secret of silk was the dowry she had created for herself.

The Very Best Porcelain

In the eighteenth century, it was the Chinese again who possessed a secret that was much sought after by other countries. No one had come up with a way to make real porcelain except the Chinese. They had been making a high-quality porcelain for hundreds of years; because it was such a different type of ware from the ordinary ceramic product, it was called "china," from its place of origin. No one else could reproduce the slick, shiny, gleaming, glassy surface.

For years, potters had been trying to penetrate the secret of Chinese porcelain, as they had tried to penetrate the secret of silk. In the eighteenth century, a French Jesuit, known to history as Father d'Entrecolles, made his way to the royal porcelain factory in the secret city of King-to-tchen. Father d'Entrecolles made a careful study of the process and sent samples of the raw material—the active ingredient not known to the West was kaolin—to France. Kaolin had actually been discovered in the neighborhood of Limoges and could be obtained in quantity. Up to that time, soft-paste porcelain had been made at Vincennes, and in 1764, when the works were transferred to Sèvres, the potters switched to hard-paste porcelain—real china.

But that wasn't the end of the story. The English sent an industrial spy named Thomas Briand to work at Sèvres underground. He in turn stole the process from the French and smuggled it into England.

The Purloined New Look

A few years ago, Mercedes, one of the largest of the German automobile manufacturers, was hit by the theft of designs for an entire new model of its expensive cars. Prints of these designs, some made for an extensive advertising campaign, were removed from the company's offices. In addition, prototypes of the new Mercedes models had also been photographed from a great distance by means of a telephoto lens and later blown up and printed.

The new models were scheduled to be unveiled at an upcoming auto show. The pictures of the plans and of the prototypes were published before the show. Thousands of orders for the new model were canceled. Mercedes estimated its loss at $600,000.

•   •   •

Other thefts of industrial secrets include:

- The secret of Scotch tape was stolen from Minnesota Mining and Manufacturing Company. The thief was in the employ of a rival manufacturer. The 3-M Company collected damages in court after the theft was proved.
- The plans for a machine used to stretch nylon fiber was stolen from

the company of its origin, Du Pont de Nemours. Because of the military importance of the theft—it happened during World War II—the FBI investigated. The thief caused his own capture when he sold the plans, samples and parts to a rival company for $3 million. The purchasing company alerted Du Pont and the thief was caught.

· The secret of casting church bells was stolen in London from one of the two companies that had been making them for centuries. The process was kept within the two families that knew them. Shortly after the theft was discovered, a new bell-manufacturing company was founded in London, proof that the thief had sold his secret.

· Not all industrial thefts are spectacular or even lucrative. One case involved the alleged filching of Procter & Gamble's Duncan Hines cookie recipe for the key trick that enables the cookies to keep soft insides and hard outsides during their grocery shelf lives. The secret? Two kinds of dough! P & G sued, claiming the secret was stolen by spies from three different firms, all rivals: Keebler Company, makers of Keebler's Biscuits; Nabisco Brands, Inc., makers of Almost Home cookies; and Frito-Lay, makers of Grandma's brand cookies.

· The secret of Aldomat, a newly developed drug to be used against high blood pressure, was stolen from the Merck Company in England in 1962. The thief offered it for sale to Parke Davis, a competitor. Parke Davis immediately warned the original company of the offer. A group from Scotland Yard went to a meeting set up by the thief at London's Russell Hotel. The culprit was arrested. He turned out to be a disgruntled employee fired by Merck for excess absenteeism. He got six months.

· In 1955, the entire advertising and promotion campaign for Crest toothpaste, developed by Procter & Gamble, was stolen from the files. The thief offered it to Colgate-Palmolive, a competitor, for only $20,000. FBI agents arrested the thief when he made the swap for $20,000 in the men's room at Kennedy Airport. The campaign he had stolen was worth millions.

19 WAYS INDUSTRIAL INTELLIGENCE IS GATHERED

Intelligence-gathering is usually confined to a number of particular sources and methods. The most obvious method of determining details of a competitor's manufacturing process or other confidential information is to hire an employee who has been dismissed or who has quit, and who possesses the information needed. The next most obvious method is to read up on the competitor's methods in published material, documents and court records and then put together the visible pieces into a complete picture.

But there are other intelligence-gathering methods, some of which border on the unethical and some of which are unethical. Those methods most executives consider to cross the ethical borderline are marked with an asterisk. They are mentioned here in the following list not as recommendations for a corporate commander, but to identify what to be on guard against:

1. disclosures of information made by a competitor's employees and obtained naturally and without subterfuge
2. information published in newspapers, trade journals or magazines or in public documents such as court records
3. material published in market surveys and consultant's reports on business trends
4. material found in financial reports and brokers' research surveys
5. information gleaned in exhibits at trade fairs, talks with competitors and competitors' brochures and promotional pamphlets
6. facts gained from an analysis of a competitor's products (reverse-engineering)
7. reported information coming in through salespersons and purchasing agents, usually obtained in talks with clients or with competing salespersons
8. factual data gained during legitimate employment interviews with employees who have worked for a competitor at one time or another
9. secrets extracted from a competitor's employee by adroit and camouflaged questioning during technical meetings or conversations at conventions or industrial meets
*10. information gained by direct observation, usually under secret and possibly illegal conditions, such as breaking and entering
*11. details gained during a phony job interview with a competitor's employee, obtained under the impression of possible employment
*12. secrets discovered during false negotiations with a competitor

in the obtaining of a license, or under the impression that a contract is about to be negotiated

13. information gained about a specific product or service by means of a hired professional investigator *(may be unethical depending on the methods used in the investigation)

14. information gained by hiring an employee away from a competitor to get specific knowhow and production secrets

*15. information supplied by bribing a competitor's supplier or employee

*16. information obtained by planting an agent of the company on the competitor's payroll

*17. disclosures of information obtained by tapping telephone conversations of the competition or by surreptitiously taking photographs or movies of the product or the assembly lines in action

*18. information obtained by stealing drawings, samples, documents or similar papers

*19. information obtained by blackmail and extortion of the competition's employees, clients or subcontractors

eleven

DEFENSE

No defense line is so strong that it cannot be dented by an enemy who is ready to expend the lives necessary to make the dent.

—GENERAL MARK W. CLARK

Defense is not a principle of war, yet it is every bit as important to understand its dynamics and its purpose as it is to understand the strategy of offense. Like Bull Halsey in the chapter heading, many military experts believe that the best defense is a good offense.

It is the proper use of defense tactics that enables a military command to go on the offense when the situation finally warrants it. In every war, even the fiercest offensive troops have spent some time in defensive postures because of some tactical situation.

The same is true of defense tactics in business.

THE THEORY OF POSITION DEFENSE

The natural tendency of any individual who expects to be attacked is to consolidate a position of defense and then hunker down and wait. Most animals and human beings tend to select a position that protects their backs and sides. Unfortunately, although the instinct is a natural one, it does not provide for the best kind of counterattack. The selection of an immobile position is a deterrent to aggressive movement in any counterthrust.

Historically, this traditional concept of defense is closely allied with the basic psychology of fortification. The ancients staked out a preserve on a piece of geography, built shelters and then fortified the shelters to keep out robbers, thieves and invaders. Defense of this type is called position defense, or fortified line defense.

Position defense is the direct opposite of siege offense—the action of an enemy in turning the principle of position defense upside down to breach it. Essentially, the aggressor says, "All right, you stay in position. I'll cut you off and starve you out!"

Through the centuries, position defense and siege offense balanced each other out. In spite of the disadvantage of position defense, it won out over the besieger as many times as it lost. The reason for the success of position defense was that siege offense took so long, cost so much money and expended the energies of so many men and beasts that it simply was not worth the effort.

However, if the aggressor was determined enough, in almost all cases of siege in history, the attacker eventually was able to invade the fortifications; it was rare that the defender was able to keep out the invader in the real hour of peril. The use of position defense, the opposite of frontal offense, is, like its opposite, the riskiest of all strategies in defensive warfare. In frontal offense, the army lines up against its opposition and slugs it out toe-to-toe. In position defense, the army hunkers down in its own bunker and faces the opposition forces head on in whatever attack eventuates.

One of the most recently remembered examples of position defense failure is the Maginot line of France, which contributed to the quick downfall of that nation against its German invaders. A brief explication of its inherent inability to keep out the aggressor points up the disadvantages of position defense.

MILITARY CASE HISTORY

THE MAGINOT LINE (1920s)

The Objective

The Maginot line was a typically French idea both in concept and in design. Of all the countries in Europe, France had one of the longest and happiest traditions of frontier fortifications: walled castles, walled cities, walled earthworks.

It was out of this historical tradition that World War I's famed Verdun line emerged. In that war, the concrete fortifications of Vaux and Douamont withstood the worst poundings of the German bombardments.

When the war was over, the French pointed to the success of this line as a reason to construct another along the whole Franco-German border.

The Strategy

Trench warfare had become the norm in World War I. This in itself was a perfect example of successful position defense. The trench was simply a hollowed-out holding area where troops could hunker down and take up a position of defense to knock down oncoming troops.

That both armies used trenches to fight was a blunt practicality foisted on them by the heavy use of artillery and cannon. Although earlier armies might encounter one another in hand-to-hand combat, slugging it out with fists, sticks, pikes, lances and knives, the armies of the nineteenth and twentieth centuries could not: The flying bullet was much too lethal a weapon.

It was France's dream in the truce after World War I to erect a barricade between Germany and France, much in the manner of the natural barricade that surrounded Switzerland and made it invulnerable to conventional military attack, and in the manner of the outmoded, thoroughly discredited and crumbling Great Wall of China.

The Tactics

In the late 1920s, the French mandated a wall along the German border, giving position defense another try, because it had worked so admirably during the Battle of Verdun. The minister of war, in charge of the military in France at the time, was André Maginot. To him went the dubious honor of giving his name to the new fortification. An updated Great Wall of China, this line of menacing aspect was made of gray concrete aggregate, with living quarters inside, gun ports along the walls, watch towers spaced at intervals and what was considered an impregnable frontal barrier.

It extended from the Swiss border of France in the east to the Belgian border in the west. It was, in effect, the ultimate in position defense, the last word in walled-in security.

When Germany had finally built up its strength to a sufficient degree, had effected bloodless coups in various European states and had decided to attack France, Hitler simply ignored the line and established his attacks on Belgium and the Netherlands. Then, when those countries fell, he occupied them and from there attacked France without firing a shot at the Maginot line.

Comment

The Maginot line became historically a kind of "fool's wall" against invasion. Some strategists blamed the mentality that created the Maginot line for the emasculation of French foreign policy, the subsequent rise of Hitler, the remilitarization of the Rhineland and all the rest of Germany's aggressive acts that led up to World War II.

· · ·

It was not only the French who dreamed of security behind a fortified line. The Germans had constructed their own line of defense, extending it along the western border of Germany. This fortification was called the West Wall or the Siegfried line.

MILITARY CASE HISTORY

THE SIEGFRIED LINE (1930s)

The Objective

France's Maginot line was built with a specific purpose in mind: to repel any invading German army. Germany's Siegfried line was not a fortification to repel invaders but a zone of terrain, planted with tank traps and other deterrents, intended to slow down rather that stop any enemy offensive.

The Strategy

The wall was built with concrete and steel fortifications that could be manned quickly and easily, but that were not laid out in an extended line the way the Maginot line and the Great Wall of China were.

Nevertheless, the line was every bit as easily subject to bypass tactics as the Maginot line.

The Tactics

The Germans did not consider the Siegfried line impregnable, nor was it built to be impregnable. However, it did hold up the Allied advance in December 1944, allowing Hitler to mount his last desperate counteroffensive, the Battle of the Bulge.

Once the bulge was penetrated and severed by the Allies, the West Wall was quickly breached.

Comment

Position defense is untrustworthy at best and suicidal at worst. It leads to self-satisfaction and overconfidence. Yet, militarily, it will certainly be resurrected in the future to lull humankind into passivity once again.

POSITION DEFENSE IN BUSINESS

In the area of business endeavor, position defense is just as dangerous, but just as tempting, as in the military. When things are going well and the money is rolling in, any successful company head tends to become complacent. It is simply not human nature to continue alert and wary in days of lush profits. The psychological syndrome involved has to do with the conviction of a successful company that its product is an invincible and irreplaceable one.

The classic "horrible" example of overconfidence is the much-examined inability of Henry Ford to see that although his Model-T automobile had made a breakthrough in the world of commerce that would change the history of transportation, he could not keep manufacturing Model-Ts forever.

Yet he tried.

CORPORATE CASE HISTORY

HENRY FORD'S MODEL-T

The Objective

At the turn of the century, Henry Ford had a dream that his close friends told him was a crazy one at best. The gasoline-driven automobile was a rich man's toy—a mechanical chariot that did not need a horse to pull it. But its ownership was confined to the rich because each car had to be engineered and constructed individually, with costly parts and labor. Ford's dream was to devise a technique of manufacture that could produce an automobile not just for the very rich but for every person in the country.

If he could ever figure out how to make the manufacture of cars as easy as the manufacture of bicycles, Ford knew he would be able to fulfill his impossible dream.

The Strategy

Ford analyzed the gasoline-powered engine and the design for the most successful automobiles at the time and decided that he could produce a car cheaply if he reduced the design and parts to the simplest degree possible. He did so. Then, with actual construction made easy, Ford hired a cheap work force to put together his very rudimentary automobile. With labor and parts costs low, he was able to price his car at a very affordable figure.

The secret of the system was the line Ford built in order to move his cars along from step to step so that each worker would only do a simple task at which he was expert. This concept became known as the assembly line technique of production. It was a phenomenal breakthrough for the manufacture of machinery of all kinds.

Ford was able to make and sell his Model-T cars cheaply, and he immediately became successful. He also became complacent. Competitors came into the market almost immediately, but Ford's Model-T was way ahead of them all. Other competitors began to refine the design of the automobile and introduced gear shifts, a self-starter and many other improvements, including luxury upholstery, superior springs and inflatable rubber tires.

Ford did not worry. He was making the car he had started with and that was good enough for him. At the peak of his success, he had a billion dollars in cash reserve—and that at a time when the dollar was worth ten times what it is today!

The Tactics

Everyone wanted a piece of Ford's market. The competition was fierce. Almost every new model intrigued the public. Ford's car began to be copied and produced for *less* than he charged. And the public was fickle. They decided they liked the changes, new designs and extra equipment featured by the competition.

But Ford held firm. He could compete no matter who tried

to take away his market. He clung to the idea that his Model-T was invincible.

Competition quickly brought Ford to the brink of ruin. Only when his company was just about to go bankrupt did he relent and let his engineers introduce different models. Eventually, in time, he diversified into expensive models, middle-priced models and cheap models—but it took a disastrous competitive war to shake him out of his complacency.

Comment

Ford illustrates the typical position defense mentality, sometimes called the bunker mentality—the tendency to hunker down and try to ignore what the opposition is doing, hoping that all the trouble will go away.

In the end Ford was forced to discontinue his own most famous model, the Model-T, and compete on the basis of those who were in the market with him. Although he hated new models and variations that were not quite as good as the original "real thing," he finally accepted the variations and became a successful competitor once again. The bunker mentality dies hard.

· · ·

Another company that was never really in danger of becoming a dinosaur before its time but was nevertheless stagnating before it shook itself into action was Armstrong Cork. Let's take a look at what Armstrong did to move out aggressively into the marketing of building material.

CORPORATE CASE HISTORY

ARMSTRONG CORK (1970s)

The Objective

Armstrong Cork came into the building construction market with a good product that could be useful to most home building contractors: a floor covering that could be shipped, shaped and laid at will, rather than slowly and laboriously put down strip by strip on the job site.

For some time Armstrong enjoyed the perfect marketing situation: It could market almost every piece of floor covering it produced. In fact, when the big do-it-yourself boom occurred after the end of World War II, Armstrong came up with new kinds of floor covering that could be laid over the original floor surface by enterprising homeowners.

However, with the do-it-yourself craze, new competitors came into the market and began to cut into Armstrong's share of the business. As the building boom after the war peaked and then began to shrink, Armstrong found that its market position was changing—and not for the better.

Although the product was unchanged and was selling fairly well, Armstrong could see that the competition might eventually become much fiercer because of the slowing down of the building market.

Its president studied Armstrong's position and decided that the company had become flanked in by a kind of bunker mentality. Armstrong Cork needed opening up to let the winds of change blow through.

The Strategy

It was obvious something had to be done, and Armstrong did it. It redefined its product. Floor coverings need not be confined to a floor in the form of linoleum, vinyl tile or carpeting—the things that Armstrong marketed. Why not apply floor covering to other areas of the house? Why not apply covering to a wall and, indeed, if to a wall, why not to the ceiling? All interior surfaces in a home were susceptible to covering.

Armstrong rethought its role in the industry and became a company supplying decorative room coverings, including walls, ceilings and floors.

The Tactics

Cork had always been the mainstay of the company—hence its original name. But now cork became just one more kind of material for use in the manufacture of room coverings. The company began experimenting with plastic-type materials for flooring tiles that could be installed easily by the do-it-yourselfer as well as the professional.

At the same time, it began looking at different kinds of ceiling tiles—acoustical types, fireproof tiles, and even ceiling surfaces that might help insulate the room below by minimizing heat escape.

In addition to ceilings, the company began looking at all kinds of easily installed wall coverings. Soon it was marketing decorative room coverings for floor, ceiling and wall, rather than limiting itself to floor coverings.

Comment

The problem of hiding behind a fortification is that hunkering down tends to stultify the mind. Survival is one thing but survival with honor is quite another. In the case of Armstrong, its own product superiority had protected it for some time from being outdone in its own province. But with the market changing, and with other competitors willing to come in and take a shot at the product, Armstrong realized that it must change with the times.

Once it began to redefine its own place in the market and see what it *really* did, then Armstrong immediately realized that there was a much wider market out there waiting for a gap to be filled. By widening its range of production and not concentrating strictly on one basic commodity, Armstrong had shaken itself out of the Maginot line syndrome and had become a viable contender once again.

In psychology, this is called "regestalting"—moving back to a distance to observe a problem as if through the wrong end of a telescope. It is human nature to settle down into a good thing, manufacturing boundaries and limitations against progressive movement that have no business being there.

There is a psychology-class story of a man struggling with a problem, and failing because of his inability to regestalt the puzzle properly.

> *THE PUZZLE:* A cricket is trapped inside a square penciled around it on a sheet of paper. It cannot escape.
>
> *THE PROBLEM:* How does the cricket get outside the square to freedom without crossing any one of the penciled lines that confine it in the square?
>
> *THE SOLUTION:* The cricket simply jumps up from the paper out of the two-dimensional plane bounded by the sheet of paper and lands outside the square on the paper—not having crossed any line! Simply put, the cricket has jumped out of a two-dimensional jail by taking to the third dimension (height).

The point is that the problem never stated that the solution lay in a two-plane system. The puzzler inadvertently and automatically *limited himself* to a two-plane system because of the fact that the drawing was made on paper in a two-dimensional manner. Regestalting is shifting around to consider a problem without its usual imagined limitations. As Armstrong did.

In this fashion, the company quite easily avoided becoming an extinct species.

THE FORTIFIED FRONT SYNDROME

Throughout this chapter it is obvious that the reason for bringing up position defense, the fortified front line or the Maginot line and Siegfried line is to point out its inherent weaknesses and its dangerous tendency to cause complacency and overconfidence in a commander who uses it, in either a military sense or a corporate sense.

In fact, in each case, the company using the position defense was jolted out of its passivity by an aggressive opponent who forced the bunker-minded standpatter to rethink, reorganize and counterattack with a new kind of approach.

It is most important that any corporate commander frequently take stock of the type of warfare he wants to wage. Is the assault aggressive enough? Is the defense strategy actually defensive enough? Does the defense posture become static and unable to compete? Is the company sinking into a Maginot line posture? Does it hide behind a Great Wall of China?

The greatest and most important part of defense is actually offense. Clausewitz wrote:

> The defensive . . . is a relative state, and consequently impregnated more or less with offensive principles. In the same way the offensive is no homogeneous whole, but inecessantly mixed up with the defensive.

Nevertheless, he pointed out that a return blow is a necessary constituent part of any defense. If the defense is not part of the attack, it is part of the act *between* thrusts. Attack, he said, is "a perpetual alternating and combining of attack and defense."

In short, the most convincing and effective type of defense is actually the type mentioned at the beginning of this chapter: The best defense is offense.

Let's take a look at a corporate commander at Heublein who ran his defense the way a good envelopment offense would be carried out.

CORPORATE CASE HISTORY

HEUBLEIN VS. WOLFSCHMIDT

The Objective

Wolfschmidt, a distributor of vodka, decided to attack Heublein, also a distributor of vodka and other beverages, staking out as much of the market as it could get by aggressive attack.

At the same time, the market was in turmoil, with new brands of vodka being marketed to test public reaction. Heublein's line of vodka included one of the very best and most firmly entrenched of all: Smirnoff. Because of extensive promotion and advertising, it was a better-known brand than almost any of its competitors.

Actually, Wolfschmidt had studied Smirnoff's vodka carefully and knew that it could produce a competitive vodka with little effort. What it would have to do was to cut the price to attack Heublein's established position in the market.

The Strategy

When Heublein heard what was happening, it immediately planned several countermoves. First it made a market analysis. The results of that analysis indicated that Wolfschmidt was selling its competing vodka, claiming it to be of equal quality, at a dollar a bottle less than Smirnoff. Heublein discovered that its own pricing was correct for the market situation; if Heublein cut the price of Smirnoff to try to knock Wolfschmidt out of the market, Heublein would begin to experience a loss of revenue.

An analysis of Wolfschmidt's cost picture showed that it would probably lose money by competing with Smirnoff at its announced price. Wolfschmidt could not continue to undersell Smirnoff by a dollar a bottle and long remain in contention.

Heublein's conclusion was that Wolfschmidt planned the low price simply to get a foothold in the market. Then it would move on, probably raising the price as business improved, or simply recouping with another more expensive liquor. Continuing to sell its brand at a dollar less than Smirnoff would be unprofitable in the long run.

The obvious and most sensible reaction for Heublein was to reduce its own price and meet the competition head-on. That would force Wolfschmidt to continue its lower price and effectively knock it out of concentration.

However, that would hurt Heublein at a time when it was marketing new products in new fields. It did not want to drop a great deal of money in a wasteful vodka war.

The Tactics

What Heublein did was to mount a double defensive counter-move against Wolfschmidt. The counterattack involved three phases:

- Instead of lowering the price of its big-selling Smirnoff, Heublein actually *raised* the price by a dollar a bottle!
- It introduced a new low-priced brand of vodka to meet the price Wolfschmidt was charging to keep the competition honest.
- It then introduced a *second* new vodka brand at a lower price than Wolfschmidt's to undercut the competition and attack it from even another flank.

Comment

Heublein had spent a great deal of effort in advertising and promoting Smirnoff as *the* vodka. Instead of lowering its price to meet Wolfschmidt's assault on the market, it simply used its image of superiority and charged *more* for its "better product"—in effect underlining the superiority of Smirnoff over the new competition.

But it fought back by introducing two new brands simultaneously, one a brand that could meet the Wolfschmidt competition head-on and force Wolfschmidt to keep the lower price for the time being, and a brand selling for less than Wolfschmidt was charging for its own new brand.

twelve

APPLICATIONS

I love it when a good plan comes together.

—John "Hannibal" Smith

The purpose of this concluding chapter is to consolidate the key concepts of this book and to discuss possible applications of these nine military principles of war to corporate situations. Interfacing military strategies and tactics with corporate strategies and tactics is a difficult thing at best, and an overview of the most important comparisons and differentiations in these principles seems appropriate.

Each of these nine principles operates at once and continuously with all the rest. Although one particular situation may feature one specific principle as outstandingly important, that does not mean that the others are unimportant.

The reverse, however, is not true. In the case of a situation in which one important principle is violated, the entire competitive struggle may be lost.

THE PRINCIPLE OF MANEUVER

Maneuver is the movement one makes to place combat power in an advantageous position with respect to the competition. This positioning action contributes materially to exploiting success, reducing a corporation's vulnerability and preserving freedom of action. Forms of maneuver include penetration, envelopment and frontal attack.

From a corporate standpoint, almost every move made on the marketing battlefield becomes a maneuver of some kind. Reducing the price of a particular product in order to meet competition head-on is a maneuver to exploit success and reduce the product's vulnerability. Invading the competition's marketing territory geographically by sending out sales troops into undeveloped terrain is another example. So is the development of a brand-new product line in hitherto virgin territory.

THE PRINCIPLE OF THE OBJECTIVE

The master and controlling principle of combat is the principle of the objective—the end to be attained through the employment of corporate action. The corporate objective determines the specific tasks assigned to subordinate units in the company. These assigned tasks, or missions, must all lead inexorably to the decisive attainment of the overall objective. Unlike military combat, corporate combat does not necessarily espouse the destruction of the competition's forces. A corporate objective is usually defined as the attainment of a superior position in a marketing or power sense, with a symbiotic posture allowing all elements in competition to remain functional and viable.

From a corporate standpoint, the typical objective in a marketing struggle is to define, elaborate a strategy for and seize a specific segment of the market by means of strategy and tactics. The objective may also be of a preemptive nature, that is, to define a particular objective in order to forestall a competitor's move to stake out territory already targeted by the corporate commander. Any objective must be clearly in mind throughout the chain of command for the objective to be won cleanly.

THE PRINCIPLE OF THE OFFENSE

Offensive action is necessary to achieve decisive results and to attain final success in any corporate action. In making a move, a corporate commander must exercise initiative and impose pressure on the competition without losing freedom of action or bowing to the competitor's will.

Generally speaking, the use of penetration tactics, envelopment tactics and frontal assault tactics in attacking a particular product market is determined by the conditions in the field of action. A corporate commander can move in directly against an open segment of the market, using the strength of a new product to break the line and consolidate a position there. Or one can perform an end run, or envelopment maneuver, by staking out a market segment on the competitor's flank, take a position there and make forays from that site. Or, indeed, one can estimate the competition's strength, deduce the market's advantages and disadvantages, pull together a superior force and mount a frontal assault against the competition.

THE PRINCIPLE OF SURPRISE

Surprise results from striking the competition at a time and place and in a manner that is completely unexpected. Because total surprise is difficult to obtain, it is not essential that the competition be taken totally unaware. the intent of surprise in the corporate maneuver is to act in such a way that the competition cannot react in an effective defensive fashion. Speed, deception, intelligence, security, disinformation and psychological ploys are all elements that contribute to effective surprise.

Surprise pertains to many different aspects of corporate combat. The shock of novelty can operate well on the marketing level with a trendy product able to produce a windfall of instant cash for the ingenious commander. Surprise can also work on the boardroom level, with tactics to forestall takeovers always at hand for the wary CEO. Surprise can also be a profitable instrument to remember in dealing with labor situations or employee relationships. The best surprise is the surprise that is not self-contained but is a preliminary move to a larger and more sustaining installation and positioning of a new product or service.

THE PRINCIPLE OF ECONOMY OF FORCE

Economy of force involves the skillful and prudent use of minimum corporate strength applied to a point other than the decisive one in order to pave the way for the application of mass force and power at the point of decision. The ability to move decisively and force costly and perilous countermoves by the competition makes economy of force such a desirable tool in the corporate arsenal.

Dozens of different types of maneuvers employ the principle of economy of force. For example, the use of a personnel raid on a competitor's upper-echelon managers is a much used and most formidable weapon. So is the use of bankruptcy statutes as a tool. With corporate combat moving out into the arena of corporate takeovers, consolidations and mergers, the ability to maneuver with economy of force in the financial jungle is a must. The use of injunctions to block a competitor's move is one type of guerrilla tactic; so is the modus operandi of effectuating a buyback in a greenmail situation.

THE PRINCIPLE OF MASS

Mass is the concentration of superior corporate power at the point of decision in a struggle between two or more corporate giants. A corporate leader with inferior forces at his command can achieve a victory by carefully selecting the point of decision and using a superior concentration of his own mass at that crucial point of interface.

The concept of mass usually involves a marketing situation, that is, the opposing line to be broken will be a line of products held by the competition. By forming all his strength into a heavy hammer punch at one portion of the market line, the able commander can smash into the opposition, breach the line and impose his will at the point of decision. Mass can also be used in research and development by the proper concentration of heavy action on the key product in the product line.

THE PRINCIPLE OF UNITY OF COMMAND

The final decision in any matter must be made by a single authority. Responsibility cannot be delegated. Unity of command assures that coordination and control are effected to attain the objective. Even though there may be lengthy conferences, compromises and doubtful assurances of cooperation, there must be little question as to who is in total control at the time of the crucial decision.

The principle of unity of command assures the proper control of a corporation, especially during a time of stress. The successful company can perform quickly and decisively when an opportunity presents itself or when threatened by opposing forces. In the corporate world, lack of unity in command often becomes the kiss of death.

THE PRINCIPLE OF SIMPLICITY

To prevent confusion and misunderstanding of orders, the corporate commander must always keep in mind the principle of simplicity. The direct, simple, well-executed plan will usually succeed. In corporate plans and orders, simplicity is essential for policies, practicalities and missions to be carried out successfully.

The extinct dinosaur syndrome is as important in corporate life as in prehistoric life. The larger a corporate structure becomes, the more apt it is to suffer from complexities and confusions that did not exist when it was small. The rush to conglomeratize is a rush to sudden extinction; it violates the principle of simplicity.

THE PRINCIPLE OF SECURITY

All levels of the corporate command must abide by the principle of security. A tight wall of secrecy around any new product. around any new marketing plan, is essential to the development of the product itself and to its eventual merchandising succéss. Security is a must if a company is to prevent surprise by the competition, preserve its own freedom of action and prevent the competition from getting information that might help it frustrate plans.

The stealing of corporate secrets, key employees and advertising campaigns by competitive companies can hurt a corporation and be costly both immediately and in terms of reduced future revenue. Tight security is essential in almost every facet of corporate life.

THE CONCEPT OF DEFENSE

Defense is not a principle of war, even in a corporate combat sense. It must be understood, however, in order to be aware of its uses and advantages. Since not even the doughtiest commander can keep continually on the offensive, there must be periods of rest. Defense is the downtime between periods of offense. A defensive posture then is inherently a temporary stance awaiting the proper time to go on the offensive. This is the only type of defensive posture the corporate commander should allow.

In a corporate situation, defense must never be used as a sheltering umbrella under which to sit out a competitive marketing struggle with a product that is considered "perfect" and "unbeatable." There is probably no such thing. Tactically, in a corporate situation, defense must be looked on as an interval between thrusts of offense in which to ponder and create a new line of attack. There is no rest in the corporate world, only the pause to breathe.

THE CONCEPT OF MORALE

Morale is the heart and soul of loyalty. It is the mental and emotional condition of enthusiasm and confidence in a worker, the spark that ignites a person to action with coworkers to perform tasks determined by corporate orders. It is esprit de corps, the instilling of psychological well-being based on sense of purpose and confidence in the future. Morale is comparable to the "heart" of an athlete as he gets "up" for a game or a contest. Morale motivates and creates enthusiasm; without morale no one, no matter how well-trained and capable, wants to move into a situation of active competition with the will to excel.

Morale in the corporate world is based on a number of specific elements: compensation, security, environment, advancement, life space, discipline, inspiration and participation. It also involves the ability of a corporate manager to train people for the effort they are about to put into a corporate move against the competition. The efficient, positively motivated, well-trained employee makes the best member of the corporate team. With an army of such employees, any commander can guide the corporation to unimagined heights.

THE KEY TO SUCCESSFUL CORPORATE COMBAT

The most successful corporate executive is the person who can effectively use any number of military concepts to run a company, increase product research and development, produce new materials to be sold, market them and create a positive atmosphere of trust and confidence not only in the company itself but in the public at large as well.

INDEX